Humming With Hopeful Things

A Little Theme of

Faith & Inspiration

With Wings

By

Connie Kerbs

Book 3 of

The Vera's Verses Series

Published by Pebbled Lane Books

An Imprint of **F.I.N.E** Reads Press

Other Titles in the Series

Whatsoever Things

A Season For All Things

Other Pebbled Lane Books
by Connie Kerbs

Paths of Fear

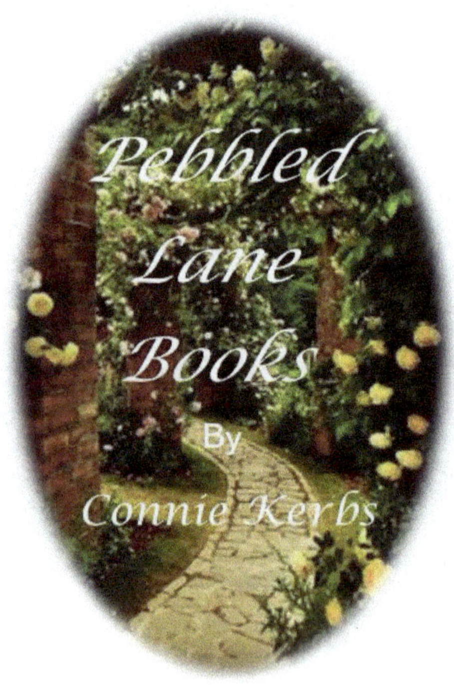

Printed in the United States of America

ISBN: 978-1-7367419-4-8

BISAC: REL006110

Religion/Biblical/Meditations/General

Nonfiction/Animals/Hummingbirds

Pebbled Lane Books: An imprint of

F.I.N.E. Reads Press

Clayton, WA 99110

www.FineReadsPress.com

www.ConnieKerbs.com

Acknowledgements

Humming owes much to a lovely grandmother, Vera, whose stacks of poetry pamphlets, books embellished with birds, and countless other beautiful things left their indelible mark.

Many thanks for the other sweet angels, patient, loving, and caring enough to expose me early on to the Good Books, inspirational poetry, beautiful, inspiring art, and the stories that would show me the meaning of not just life – but the living of it to the fullest: a life ever humming with a brightness of hope, thus a zeal for life itself and all that it offers.

Gratitude is not only the greatest of virtues, but the parent of all the others.

Marcus Tullius Cicero

Dedication

To He who hath buoyed me up, lifted me up, and filled me up. He who hath, time and again, overflowed my cup with that sublime blend of grace, gratitude, and exquisite joy, as described by these eloquent words penned over a thousand years ago:

Could we with ink the ocean fill,
Were the heavens of parchment made,
Were every stalk on earth a quill,
And every man a scribe by trade;
To write the love of God above,
Would drain the ocean dry;
Nor could the scroll Contain the whole,
Though stretched from sky to sky

Meir Ben Isaac Nehorai

Introduction

Heroes come in many shapes and sizes, and their stories can be filled with valiant adventures, formidable foes, and powerful, influential circumstances through which they have positively impacted others. Often many others.

Here I want to talk about a different kind of hero – but one, none-the-nonetheless. This hero is unassuming. They would likely never think of themselves as such, (as a hero or heroic) not alone call themselves that. It would literally be the furthest thing from their mind – and heart. Which is part of what makes them so admirable – their genuine humility. They simply just do what they do, are what they are; with no pretention, or expectation of acknowledgement. No need for credit. In fact, these heroes sincerely, inwardly, outwardly, and every way in between, prefer anonymity.

This class of hero I am talking about often grieves in private, silently, unnoticed, breaching extraordinary and extremely difficult obstacles. They face hurdles most people can only imagine in their worst nightmares. They stand up to, with dignity, and a silent, beyond admirable courage – to circumstances that would crush most of us mind, body, and spirit. They find the flowers blooming – in proverbial war zones. They see deep beauty where most only find superficial contempt. They appreciate the good in terrible, unthinkable circumstances. They smile and laugh through things most of us would not be able to endure, not alone well, or with any kind of grace, as they just do.

I have had the distinct blessing of knowing firsthand a few of these heroes. Some born into adversity from the very, VERY beginning, others plunged into it a little later – the details of which would traumatize the average person just from learning of it.

Foster parenting is like that. You have the privilege of brushing with heroes on a regular basis. Children, whose next-level resilience is the stuff of legends and fables – if only their stories could be told. Typically, they can't because of confidentiality, privacy, and just that good old- fashioned respect and confidentiality that good humans give each other.

There is one story, I will just hint of here, to which this book is dedicated: a daughter, who has blessed us beyond description with her living, and surviving tragic circumstances, against all odds. Her whole life has been virtually one long, wide, and deep series of miracles, that we have had the exquisite privilege of observing and being a part of, from the inside out.

It wasn't an experience that we could prepare for, though we were *prepared.* It wasn't an experience we knew exactly what to do with – especially in the beginning. But we figured it out, the best we could – through many other layers of miracles as we too were tempered in the fire along with her – at least to a point.

Just to be clear, though – there is only one hero, rather, heroine in this story. Our sweet Avah. It is to her, her valiant overcoming of unthinkable injuries, her sheer will to live against all odds, and her fiery, angelic spirit that has shown us what courage and hope is beyond explanation or understanding – it is to her that this work is devoted.

Simply put, our hearts were transformed from the very beginning of this unlikely, unexpected, match – an Adoption made possible only by, and through, a Higher Hand, weaving an intricate, Divine Design. This heart and soul transformation of ours continues, as, at this work's first publication, we celebrate a glorious, but once unimaginable 12th birthday with this extraordinary daughter. She, a precious little girl, who through no fault of her own, as an innocent infant, was initially put on a trajectory that was to disallow even her tender first birthday.

Also, all the miraculous, even magical space between then and now has flown by, not too unlike the flutter of hummingbird wings; hard to ascertain, or pin down to specifics, but still as tangible – and beautiful as anything. It has all been beyond memorable and poignantly lifechanging for all of us. Indeed, it has been a season, an epoch even, which has taught us more about love, miracles, gratitude, and that most transcendent thing called *hope* – than we ever imagined we would – or could, comprehend.

And so, it is my sincerest aspiration that this project will capture a glimmer of some of these indescribable reelings, feelings, and healings we have been so fortunate to know through this most beautiful and inspiring experience we call *Avah*. Also, it is a heart-wish that this tribute of stories, poetry, and verse will, somehow, both preserve *and* share all the above in meaningful, helpful ways for others.

And so, we wish a happy, happy, *miraculous,* 12th birthday to our dear Avah. It is this extraordinary occasion that gives us pause and has been the inspiration for this book as we search for ways to express our gratitude - which is to us as impressive, palpable, and promising as fluttering *hummingbird wings*.

Gratefully Yours,
Connie Kerbs

Contents

Foreward

In our fast-paced lives, amidst challenges and uncertainties, we seek solace, inspiration, and a glimmer of hope. "Humming with Hopeful Things" by Connie Kerbs is one such treasure - a profound collection of wisdom in the enduring themes of God, faith, and hope.

This remarkable devotional invites readers on a transformative journey guided by Connie's gentle wisdom, rooted in her steadfast faith in God. Just as these tiny birds symbolize resilience and perseverance, Connie's words ignite dormant dreams and infuse our spirits with a renewed sense of hope, reminding us that even in the bleakest moments, God's light and beauty await.

Authenticity is at the heart of "Humming with Hopeful Things." Connie effortlessly weaves wisdom, scriptures, quotes, and stories that touch readers from all walks of life. With heartfelt compassion and a faith forged by that thing called *trial by fire,* she uses her experiences as a devoted wife, mother, foster and adoptive parent to invite readers to embrace both the joys and challenges of their own journeys, encouraging them to find strength, resilience, and that infallible hope we all need in the end.

This devotional is a beacon of hope, a refuge for weary souls seeking solace in the arms of faith. The wisdom within these pages inspires us to embrace our journeys, lean on our faith, and hold onto hope with unyielding determination, knowing that God's plans for us are filled with goodness and purpose.

Delve into "Humming with Hopeful Things" and let its beauty, profound insights, and inspirational words ignite a personal journey of hope rooted in your relationship with God. May its impact bring you solace, reminding you that God's light shines through every circumstance, and with faith and hope, you possess the strength to overcome any obstacle.

I am delighted to introduce you to this captivating collection of wisdom and encouragement, where hope flutters and brings solace to your soul. Open your heart, embrace its words, and let the humming of hope reverberate within your being.

May this book serve as a steadfast companion on your journey of faith and light, guiding you toward that Higher Hope found in the embrace of God's Love.

-Margaret Poling
Writer and Developmental Editor

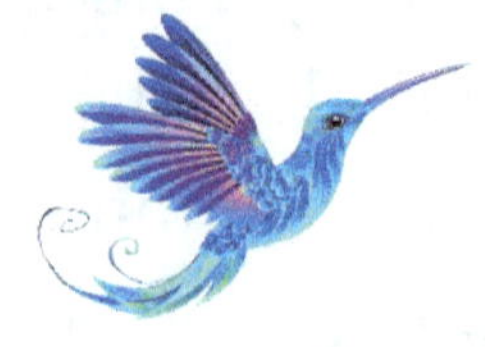

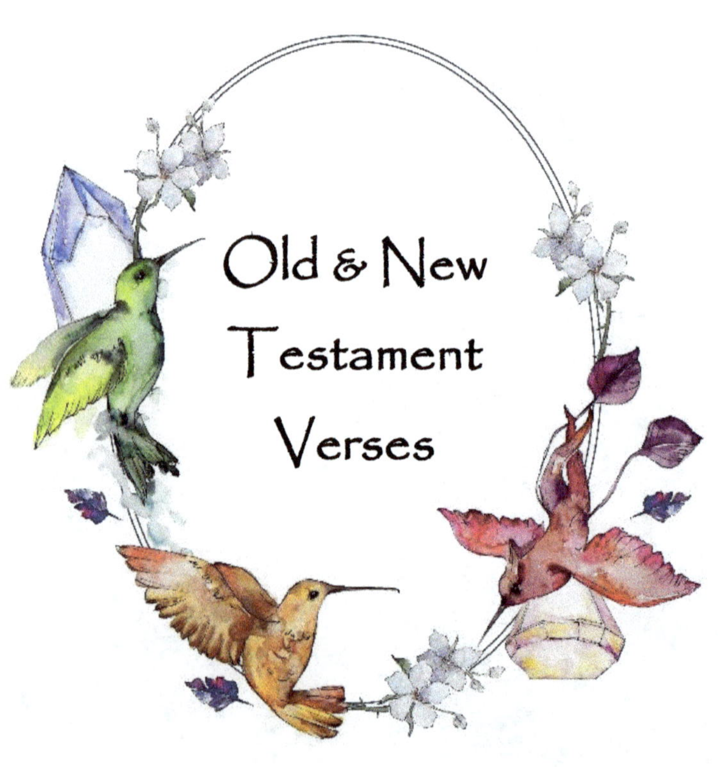

Old & New Testament Verses

Psalm 39:7

"And now, Lord, what wait I for?
My hope is in thee."

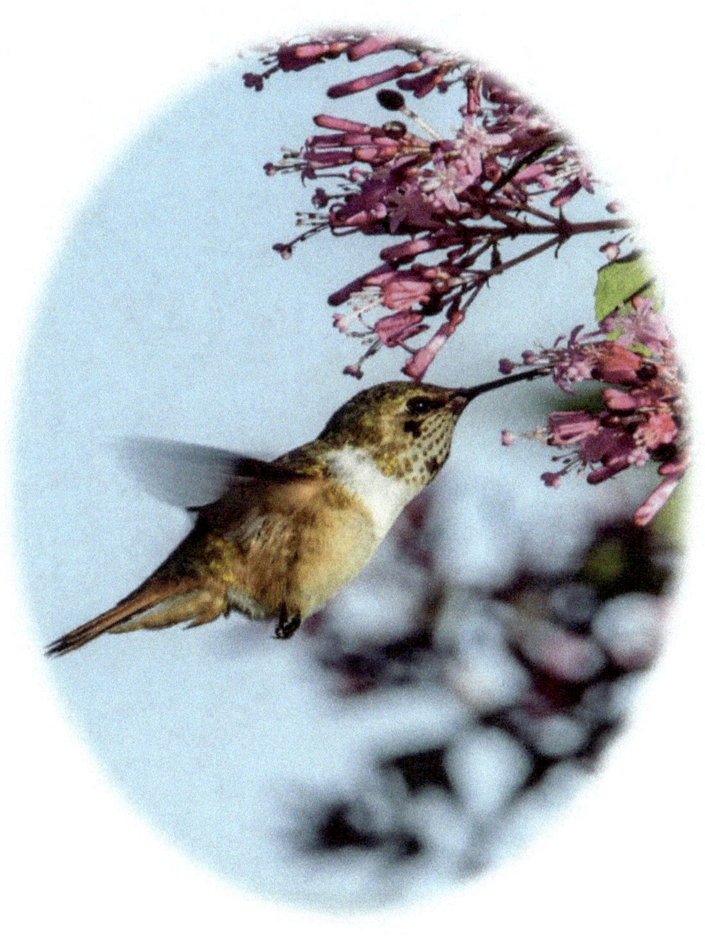

Jeremiah 31:17

And there is hope in thine end, saith the LORD, that thy children shall come again to their own border.

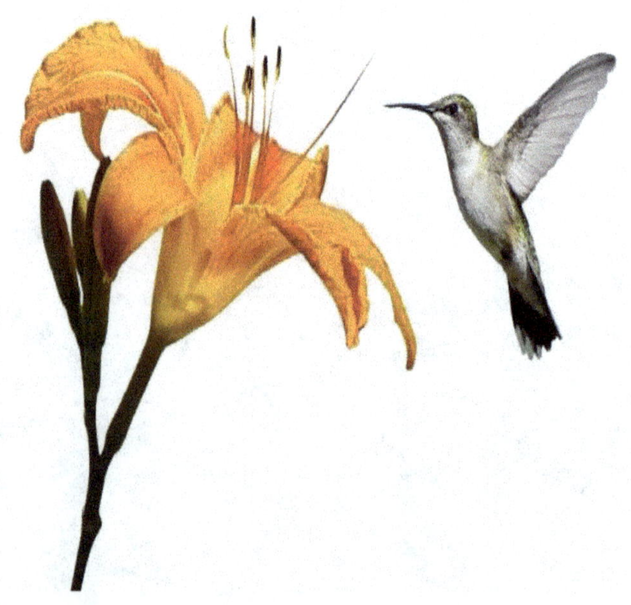

Lamentations 3:21

This I recall to my mind,
Therefore I have hope.

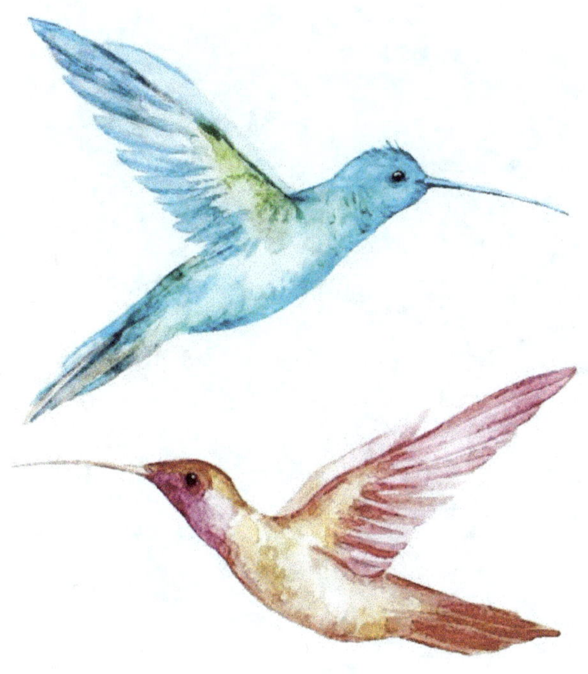

Psalm 31:24

Be of good courage, and he shall
strengthen your heart,
all ye that hope in the LORD.

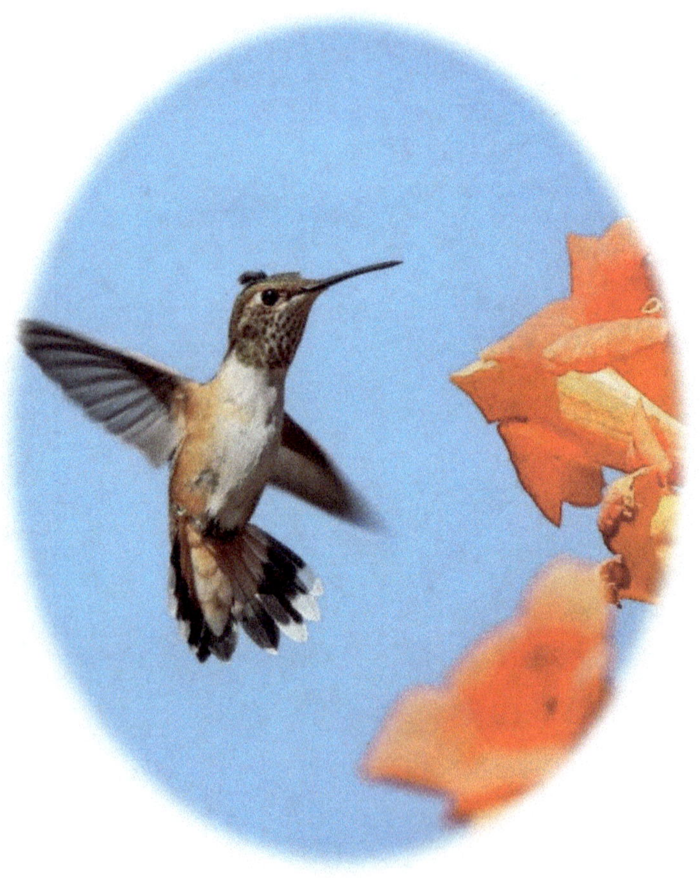

Psalm 9:18

For the needy shall not always be forgotten: the expectation of the poor shall not perish forever.

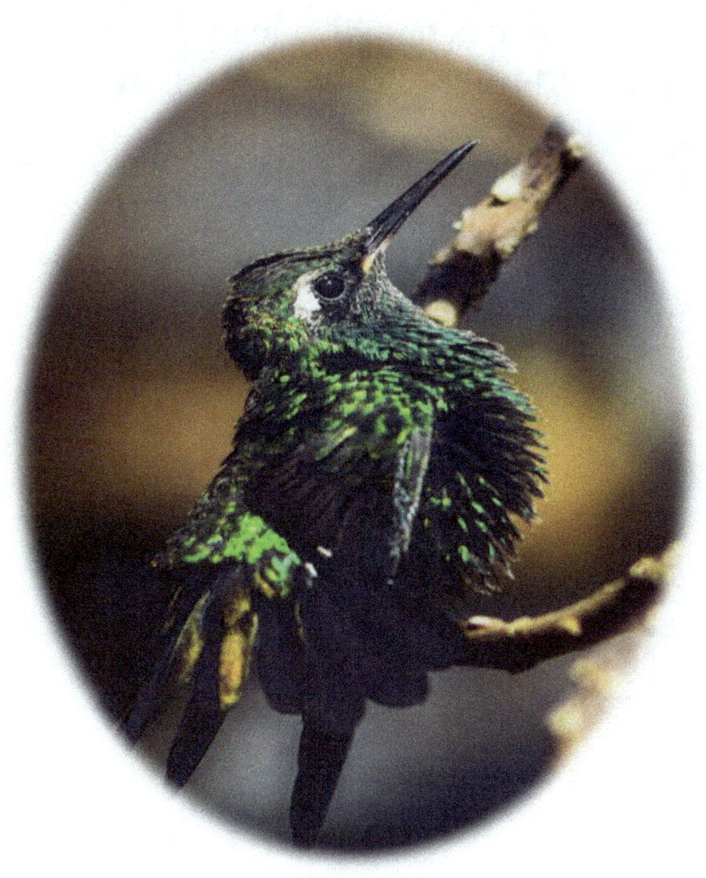

Lamentations 3:19-21

Remembering mine affliction
and my misery,
the wormwood and the gall.
My soul hath them still in remembrance,
and is humbled in me.
This I recall to my mind,
therefore have I hope.

Lamentations 3:25-26

The LORD is good unto them that wait for him, to the soul that seeketh him.
It is good that a man should both hope and quietly wait for the salvation of the LORD.

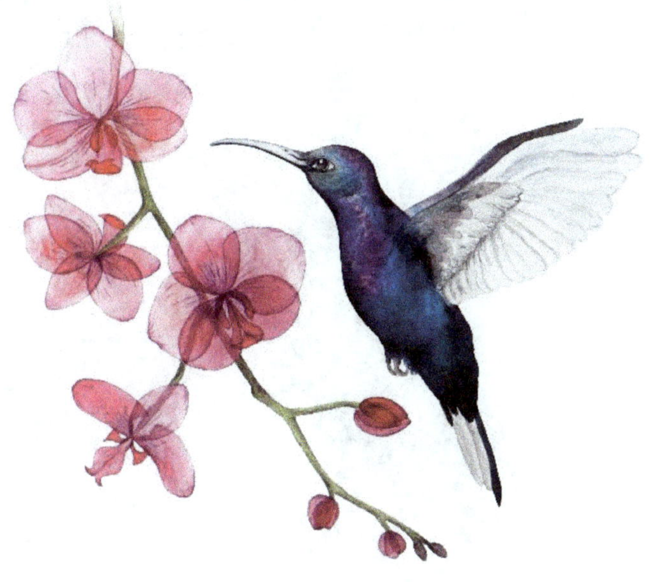

Lamentations 3:22-24

It is of the LORD'S mercies
that we are not consumed,
because his compassions fail not.
They are new every morning:
great *is* thy faithfulness.
The LORD *is* my portion, saith my soul;
therefore will I hope in him.

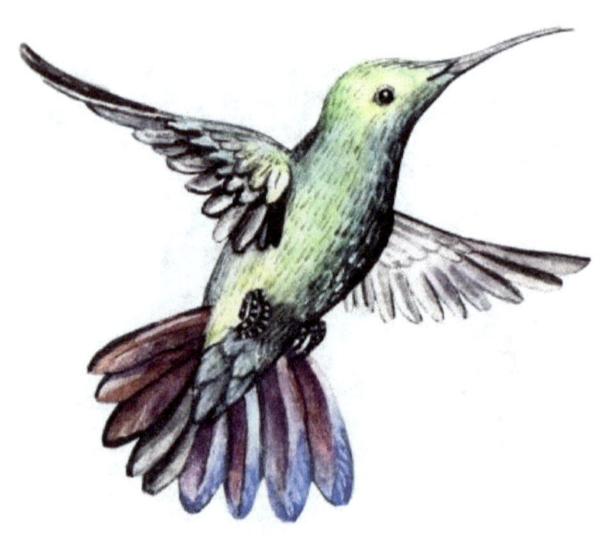

Isaiah 40:31

But they that wait upon the LORD
shall renew their strength;
they shall mount up with wings as eagles;
they shall run, and not be weary;
and they shall walk, and not faint.

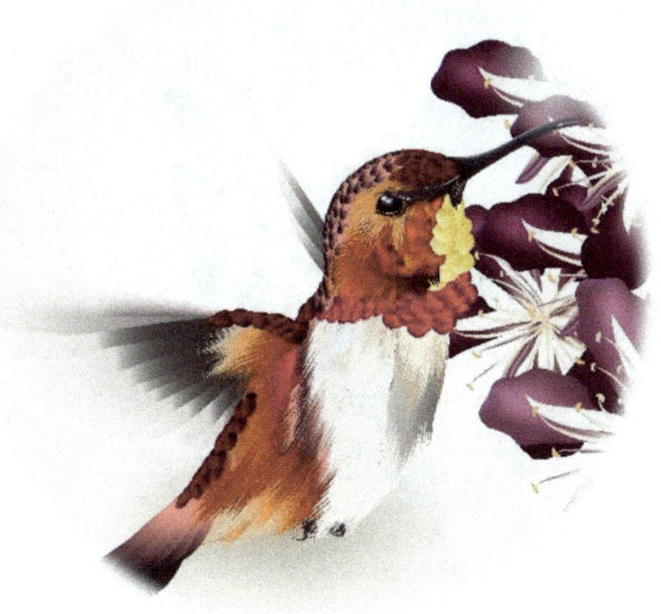

Proverbs 19:18

Chasten thy son while there is hope, and let not thy soul spare for his crying.

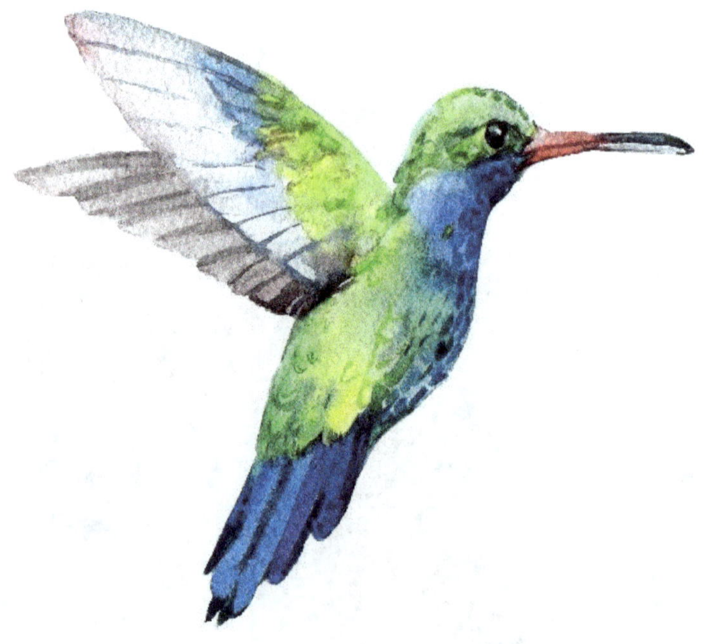

Job 4:4

Thy words have upholden him that was falling, and thou hast strengthened the feeble knees.

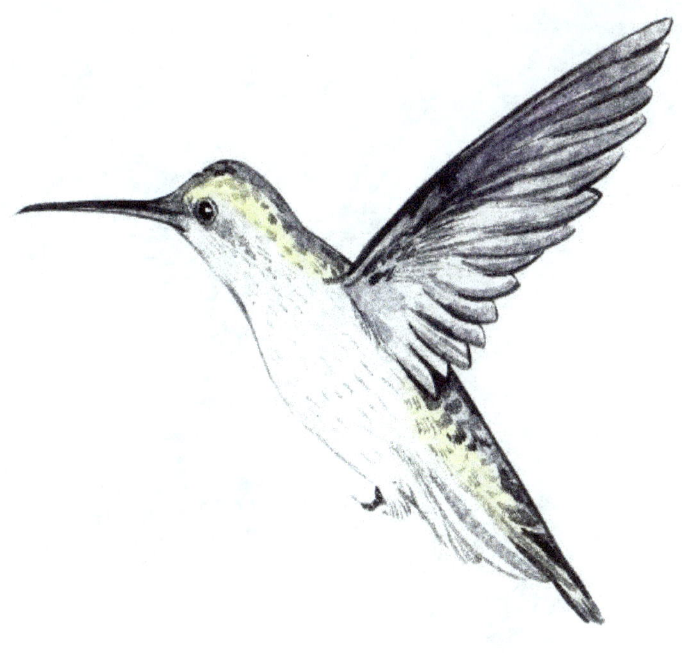

Job 14:7

For there is hope of a tree, if it be cut down,
that it will sprout again, and that the
tender branch thereof will not cease.

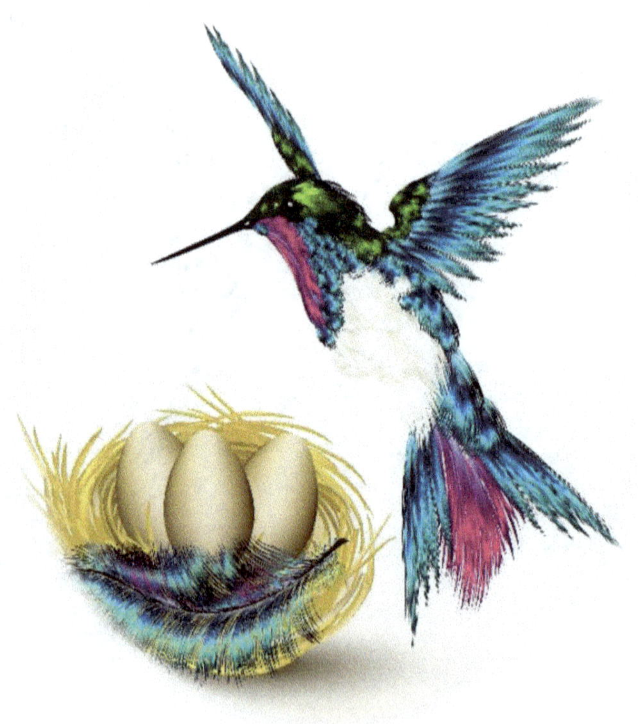

Psalm 33:20-22

Our soul waiteth for the LORD:
he is our help and our shield.
For our heart shall rejoice in him,
because we have trusted in his holy name.
Let thy mercy, O LORD, be upon us,
according as we hope in thee.

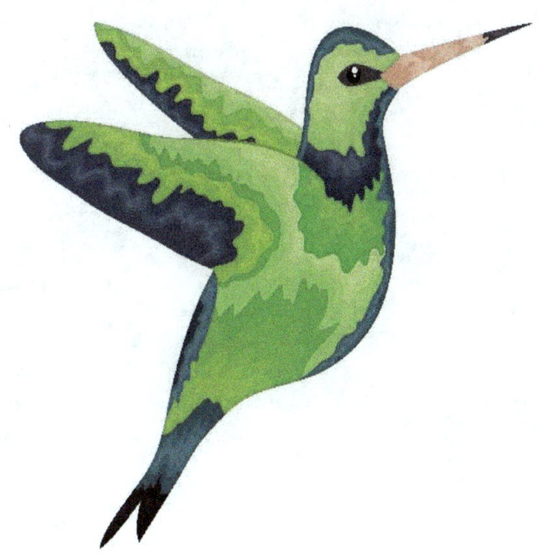

Psalm 38:15

For in thee, O LORD, do I hope: thou wilt hear, O Lord my God.

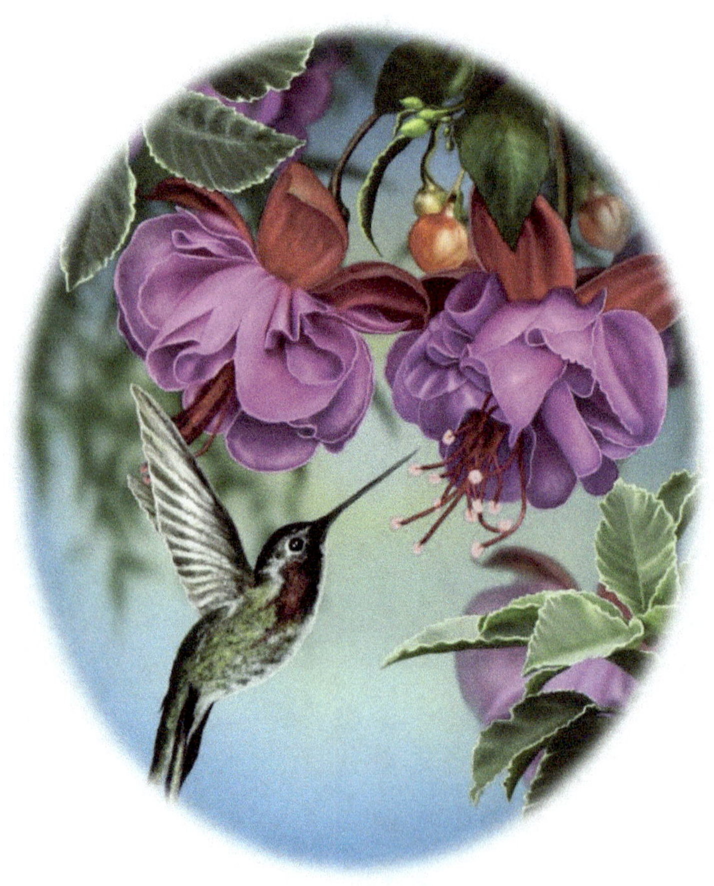

Psalm 38: 21-22

Forsake me not, O LORD: O my God, be not far from me.
Make haste to help me, O Lord my salvation.

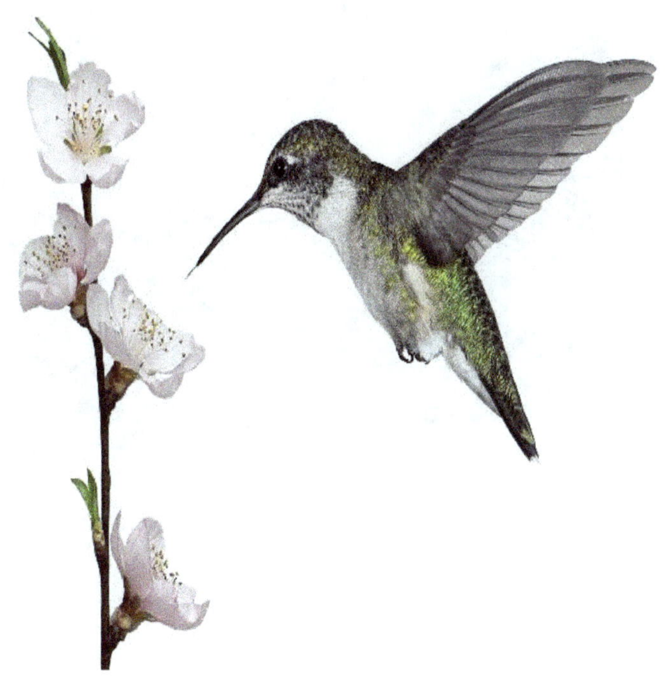

Psalm 71:1-3

In thee, O LORD, do I put my trust: let me never be put to confusion.
Deliver me in thy righteousness and cause me to escape: incline thine ear unto me, and save me.
Be thou my strong habitation, whereunto I may continually resort: thou hast given commandment to save me; for thou art my rock and my fortress.

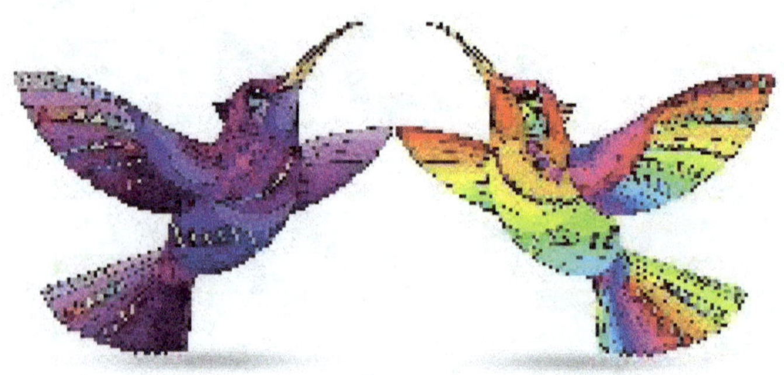

Psalm 71:4-5

Deliver me, O my God, out of the hand of
the wicked, out of the hand of the
unrighteous and cruel man.
For thou art my hope, O Lord GOD: thou
art my trust from my youth.

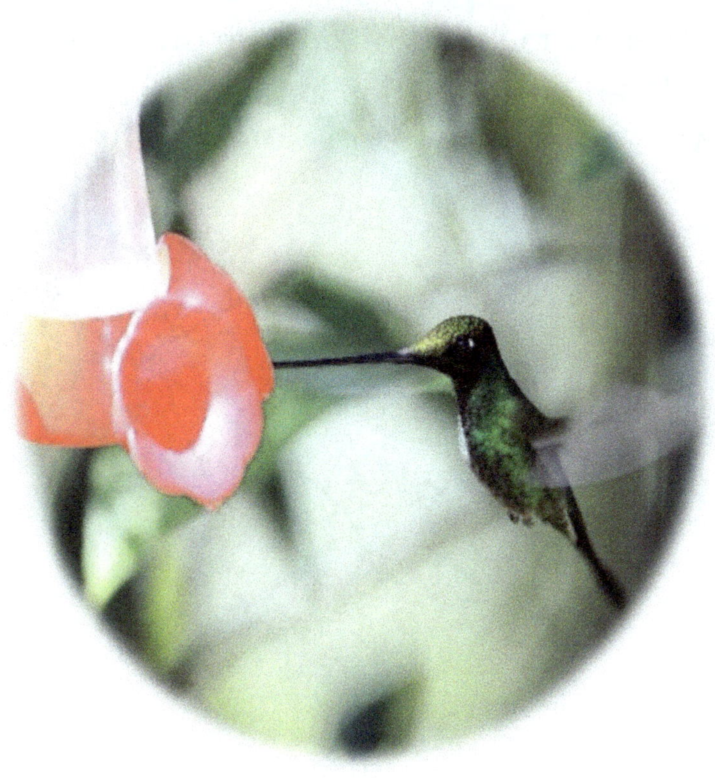

Psalm 71:6-8

By thee have I been holden up from the
womb: thou art he that took me out of my
mother's bowels: my praise shall be
continually of thee.
I am as a wonder unto many;
but thou art my strong refuge.
Let my mouth be filled with thy praise
and with thy honour all the day.

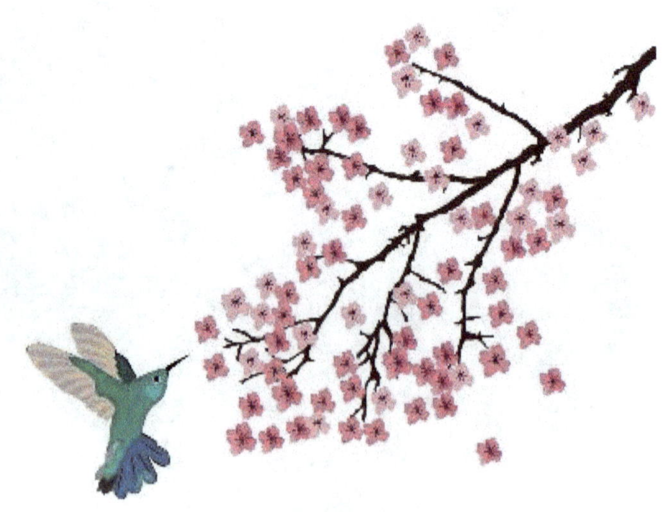

Psalm 71:14

But I will hope continually, and will yet praise thee more and more.

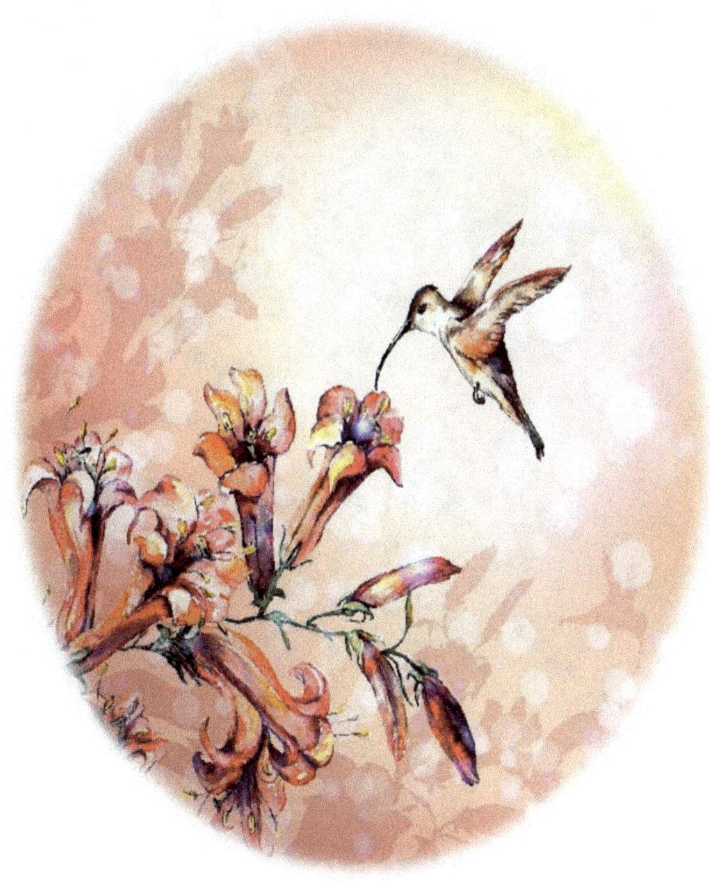

Psalm 71:16

I will go in the strength of the Lord GOD…

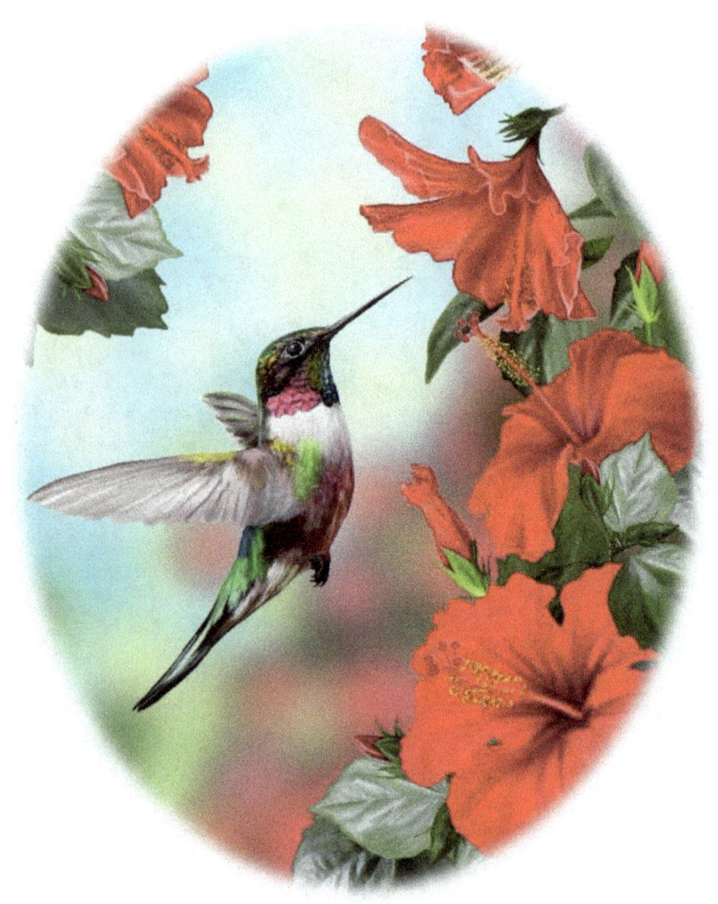

Psalm 71: 17

O God, thou hast taught me from my youth: and hitherto have I declared thy wondrous works.

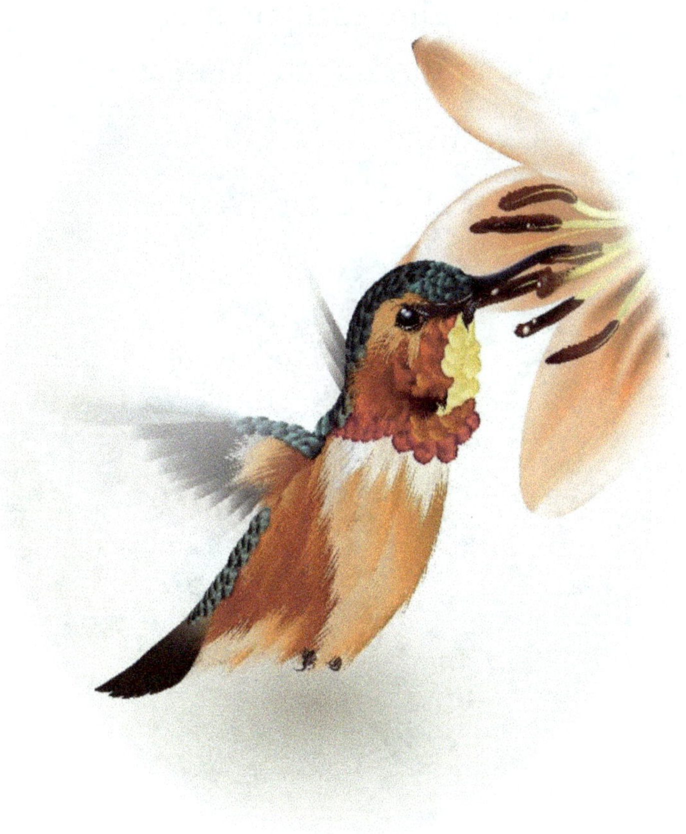

Psalm 71:20

Thou, which hast shewed me great and
sore troubles, shalt quicken me again,
and shalt bring me up again
from the depths of the earth.
Thou shalt increase my greatness,
and comfort me on every side.

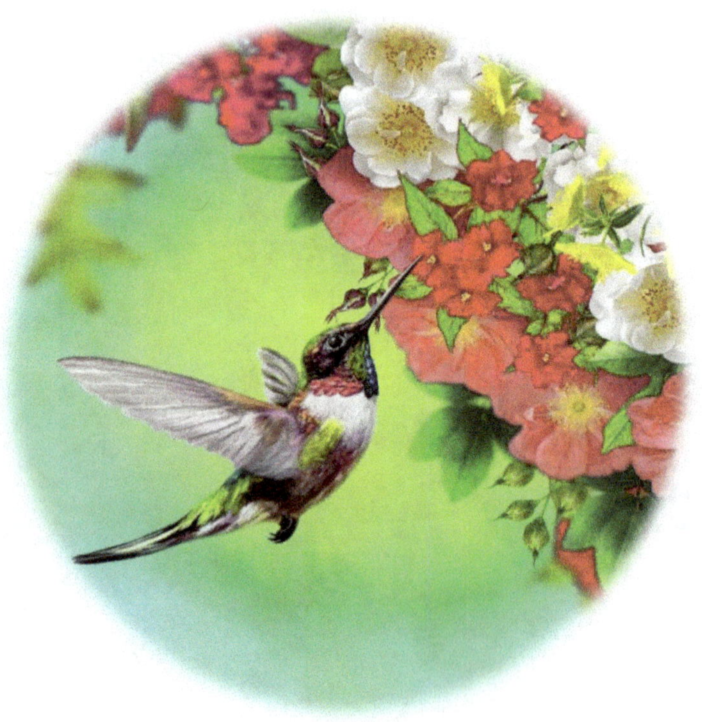

Psalm 78:6-7

That the generation to come might know them, even the children which should be born; who should arise and declare them to their children:
That they might set their hope in God, and not forget the works of God, but keep his commandments:

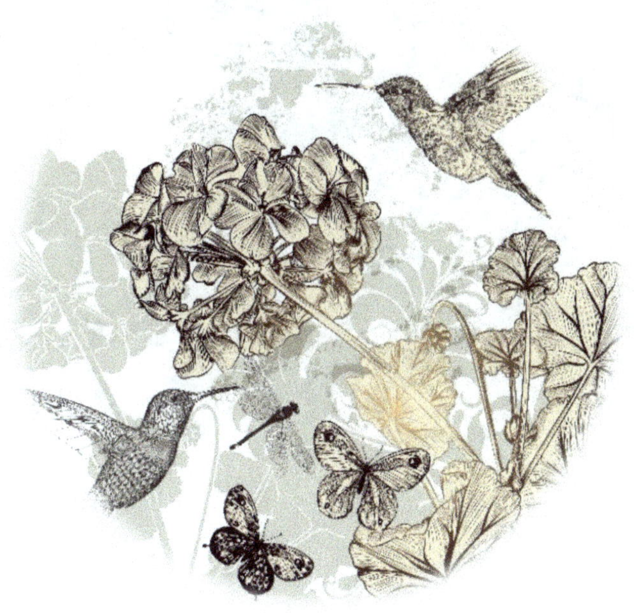

Psalm 119:2

Blessed are they that keep his testimonies, and that seek him with the whole heart.

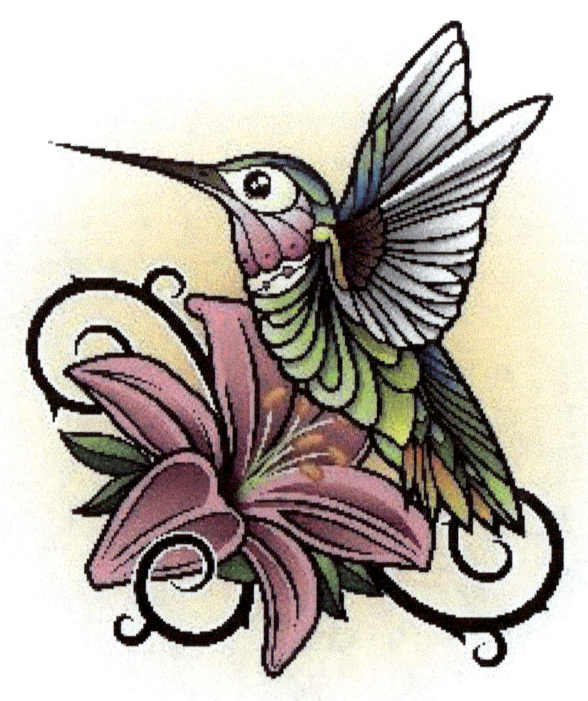

Psalm 119: 10 – 11

With my whole heart have I sought thee:
O let me not wander from
thy commandments.
Thy word have I hid in mine heart,
that I might not sin against thee.

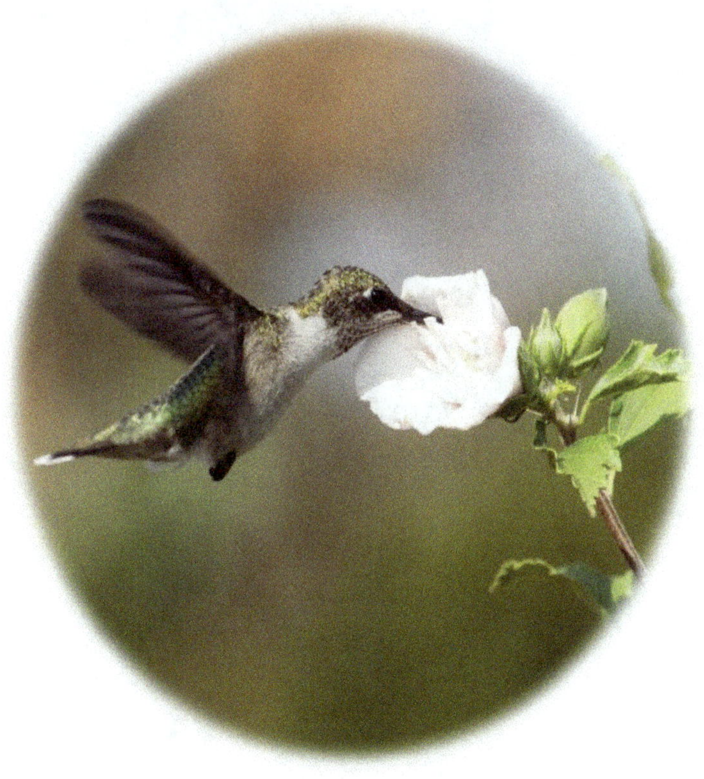

Psalm 119: 12-14

Blessed art thou, O LORD:
teach me thy statutes.
With my lips have I declared all the
judgments of thy mouth.
I have rejoiced in the way of thy
testimonies, as much as in all riches.

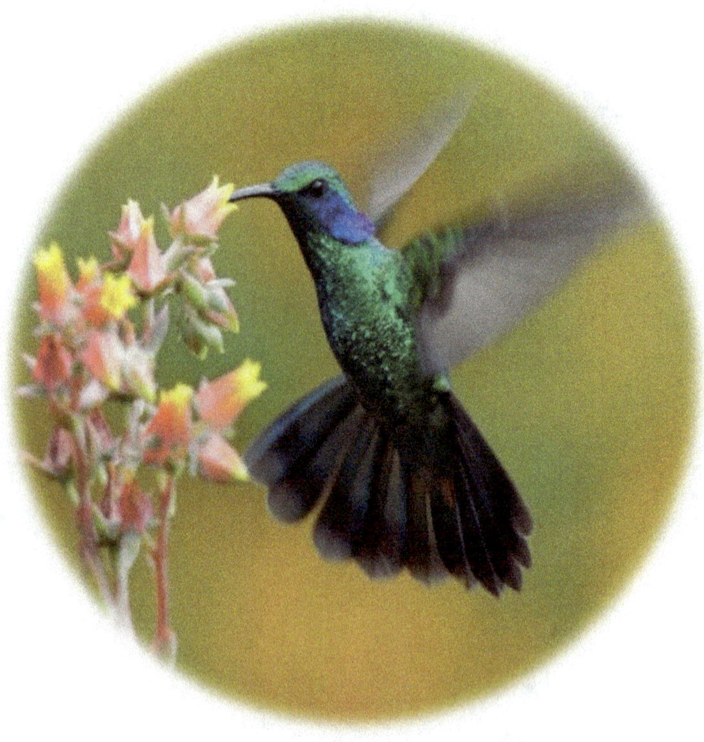

Psalm 119: 15-16

I will meditate in thy precepts
and have respect unto thy ways.
I will delight myself in thy statutes:
I will not forget thy word.

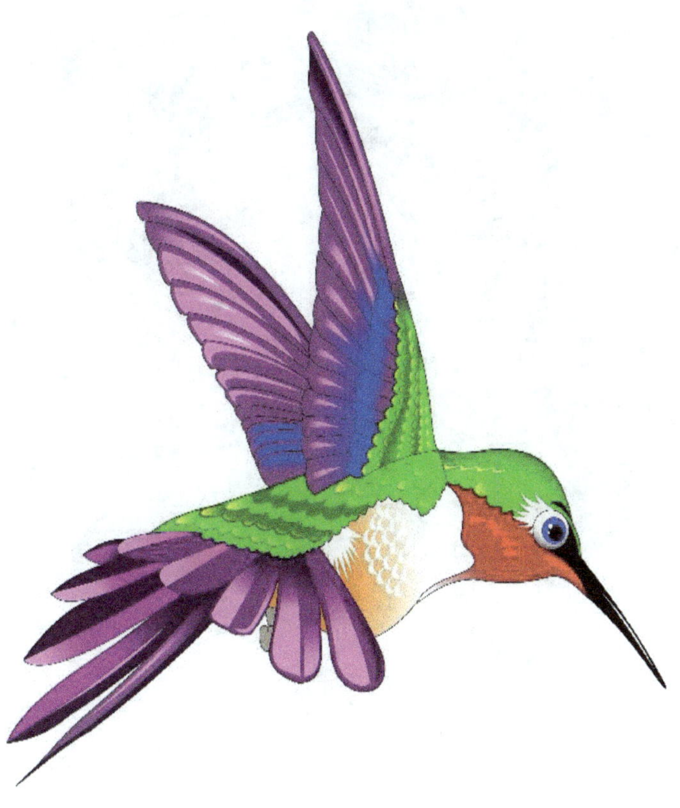

Psalm 119: 28-29

My soul melteth for heaviness:
strengthen thou me according
unto thy word...grant me
thy law graciously.

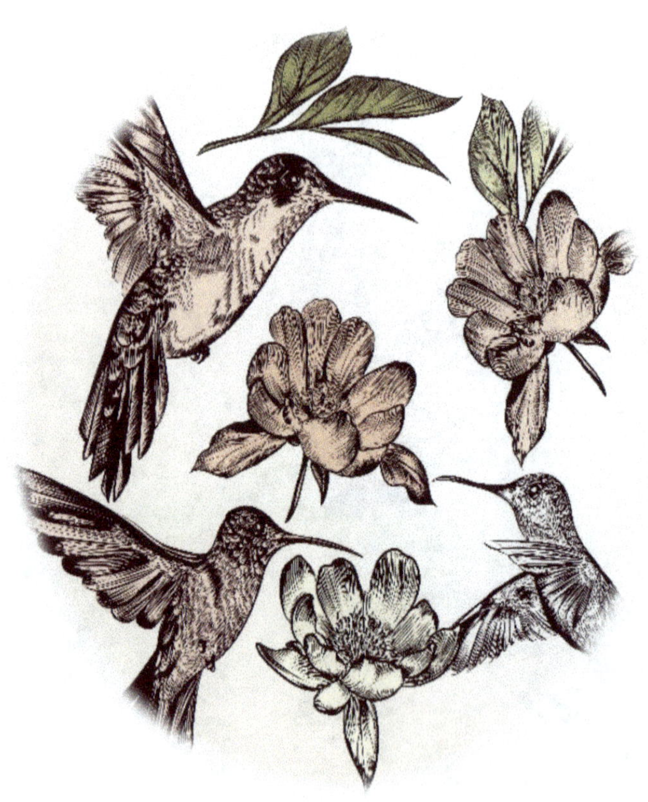

Psalm 119:33-35

Teach me, O LORD, the way of thy
statutes; and I shall keep it unto the end.
Give me understanding, and I shall
keep thy law; yea, I shall observe it
with my whole heart.
Make me to go in the path of
thy commandments; for therein
do I delight.

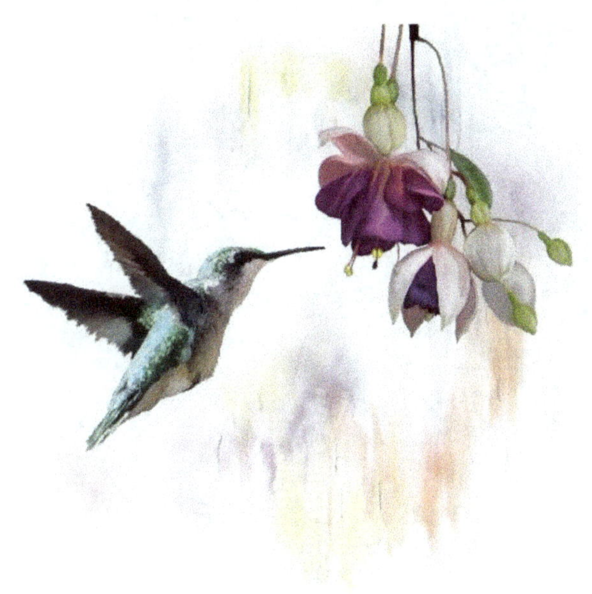

Psalm 119: 36-37

Incline my heart unto thy testimonies,
and not to covetousness. Turn away mine
eyes from beholding vanity;
and quicken thou me in thy way.

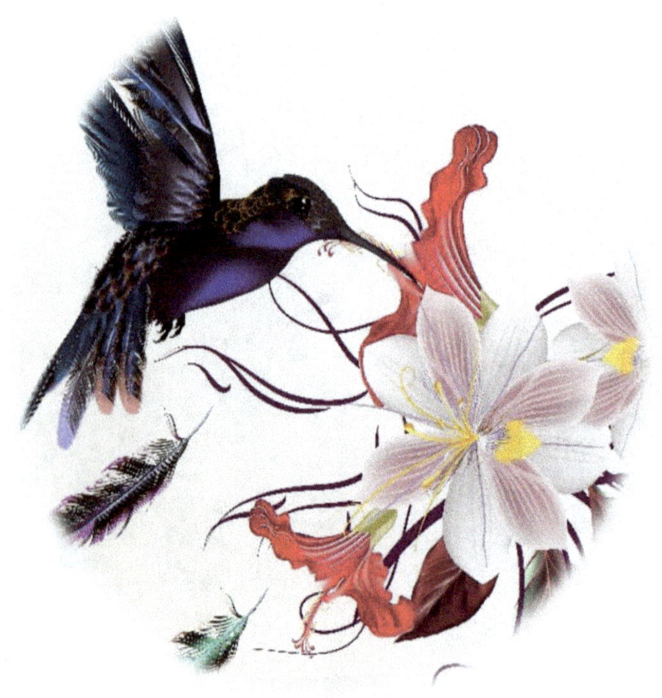

Psalm 119:40

Behold, I have longed after thy precepts: quicken me in thy righteousness.

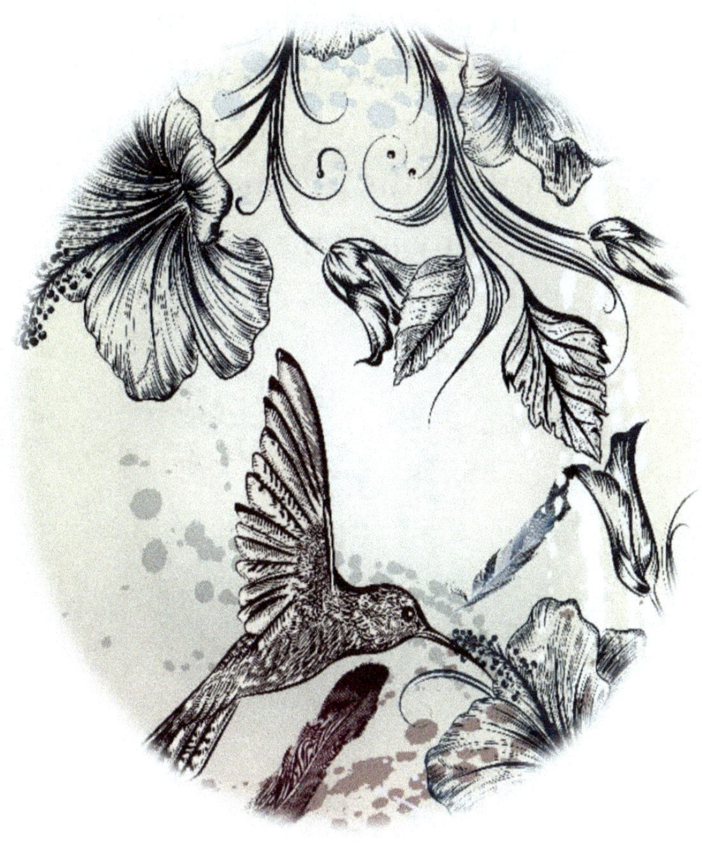

Psalm 119: 41-43

Let thy mercies come also unto me,
O LORD, even thy salvation,
According to thy word.
So shall I have wherewith to answer
him that reproacheth me:
for I trust in thy word.
And take not the word of truth utterly
out of my mouth; for I have hoped
in thy judgments.

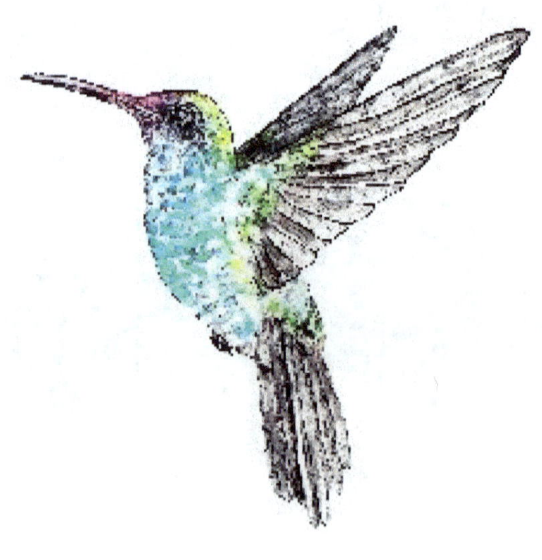

Psalm 119: 44-47

So shall I keep thy law continually
for ever and ever.
And I will walk at liberty:
for I seek thy precepts.
I will speak of thy testimonies also
before kings, and will not be ashamed.
And I will delight myself
in thy commandments,
which I have loved.

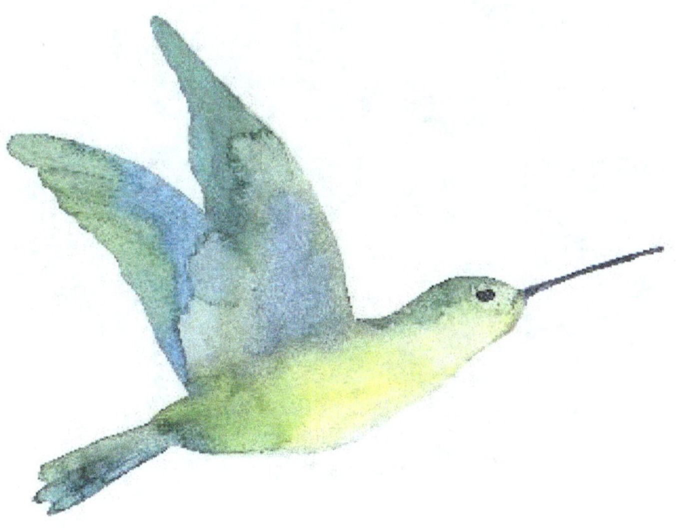

Psalm 119: 48-49

My hands also will I lift up unto thy commandments, which I have loved; and I will meditate in thy statutes. Remember the word unto thy servant, upon which thou hast caused me to hope.

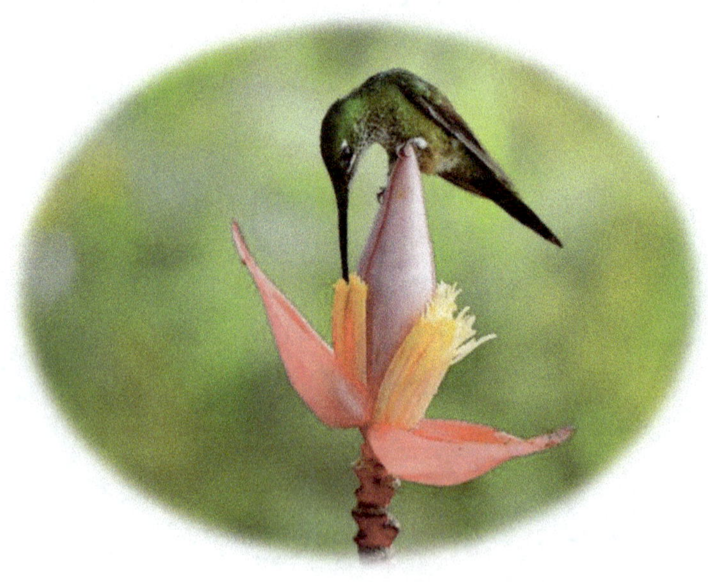

Psalm 119:81

My soul fainteth for thy salvation:
but I hope in thy word.

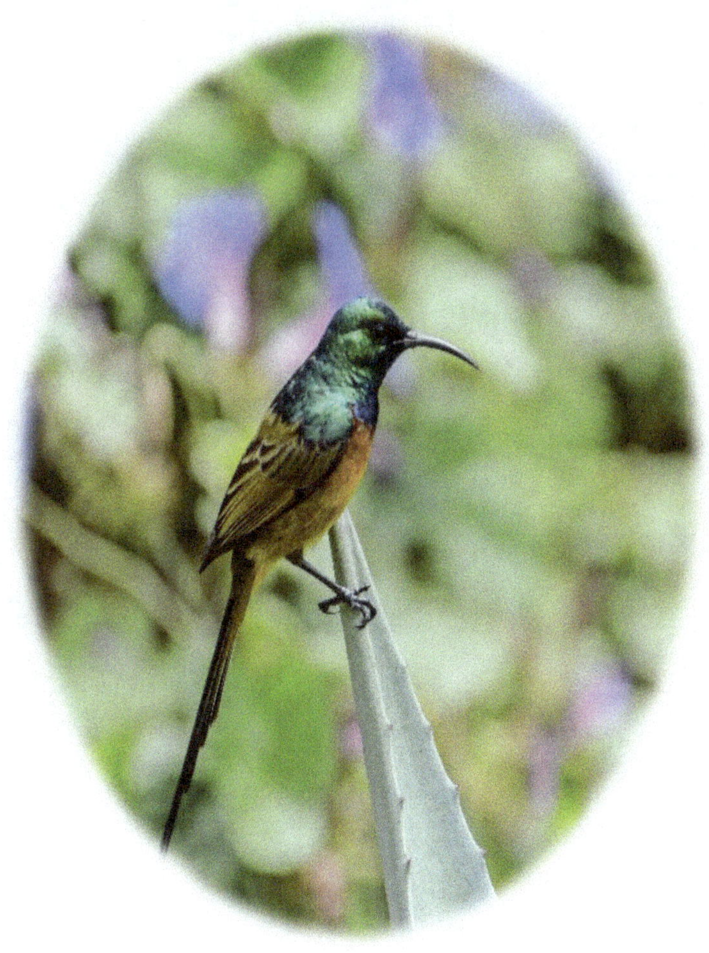

Psalm 119:94

I am thine, save me;
for I have sought thy precepts.

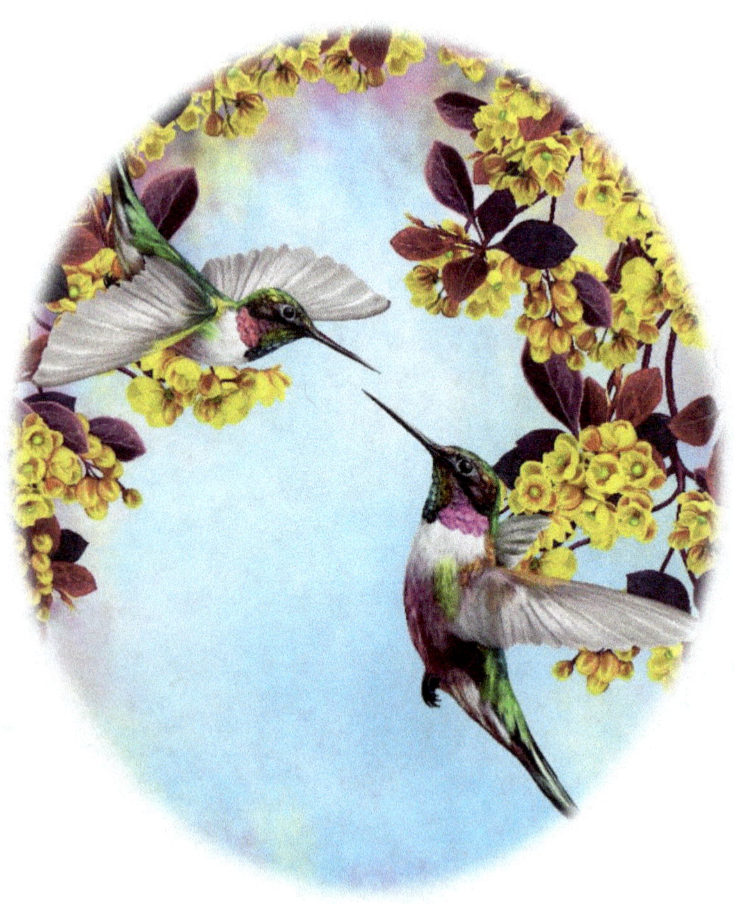

Psalm 119:105

Thy word is a lamp unto my feet,
and a light unto my path.

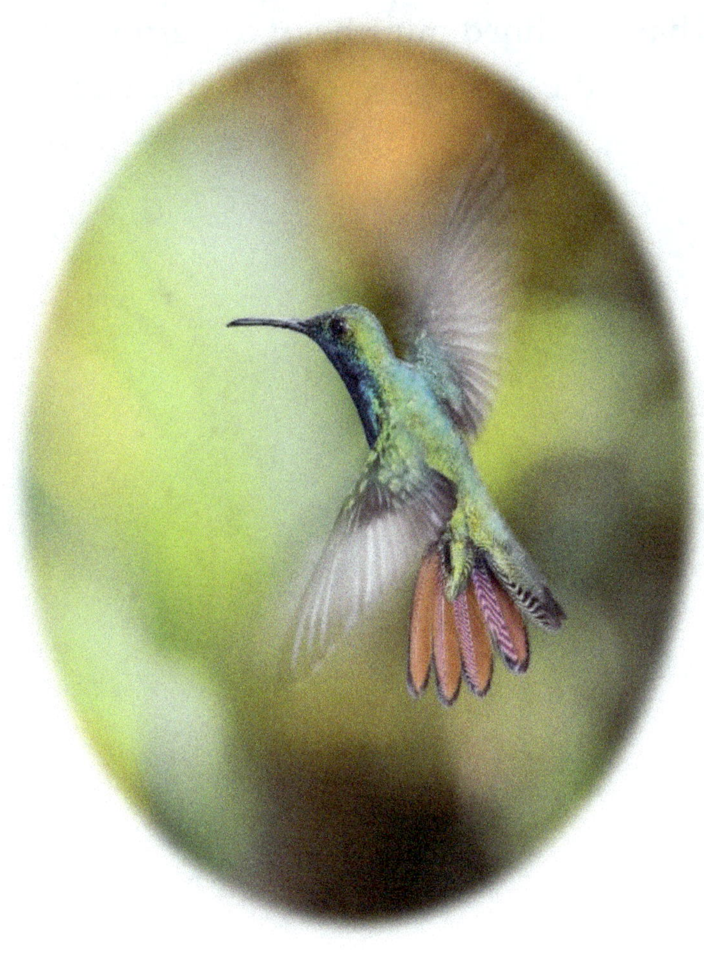

Psalm 119:111-112

Thy testimonies have I taken as an
heritage forever: for they are
the rejoicing of my heart.
I have inclined mine heart to perform thy
statutes always, even unto the end.

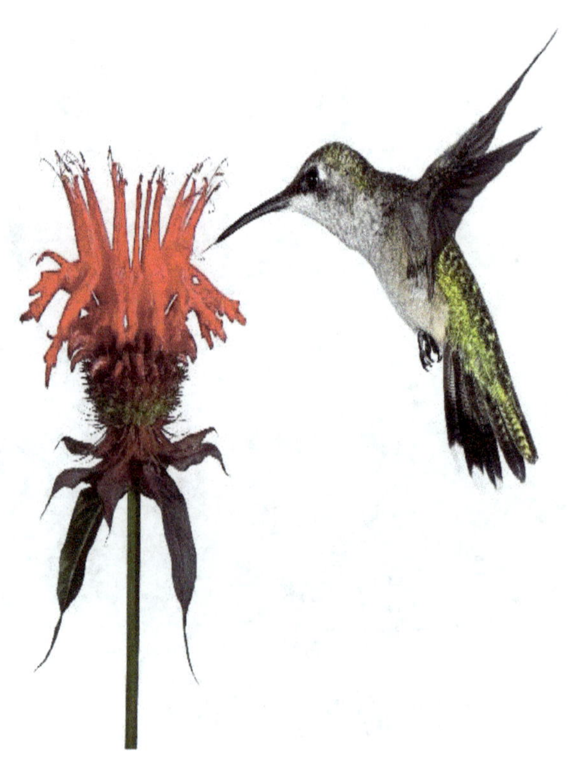

Psalm 119:116

Uphold me according unto thy word, that I may live: and let me not be ashamed of my hope.

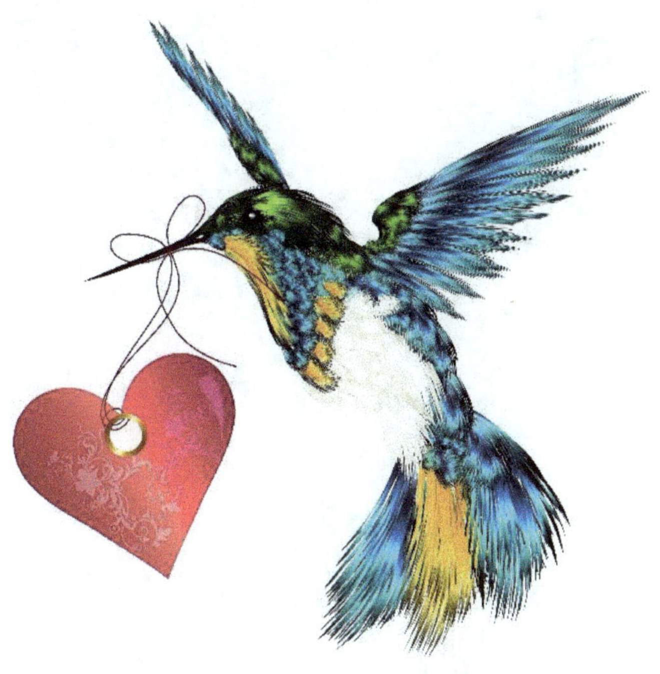

Psalm 119:114

Thou art my hiding place and my shield:
I hope in thy word.

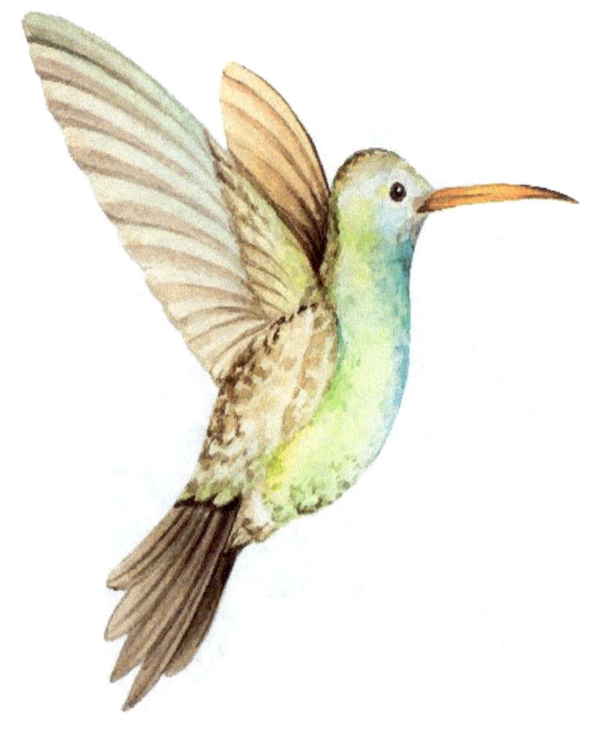

Psalm 119:129-130

Thy testimonies are wonderful:
therefore doth my soul keep them.
The entrance of thy words giveth light; it
giveth understanding unto the simple

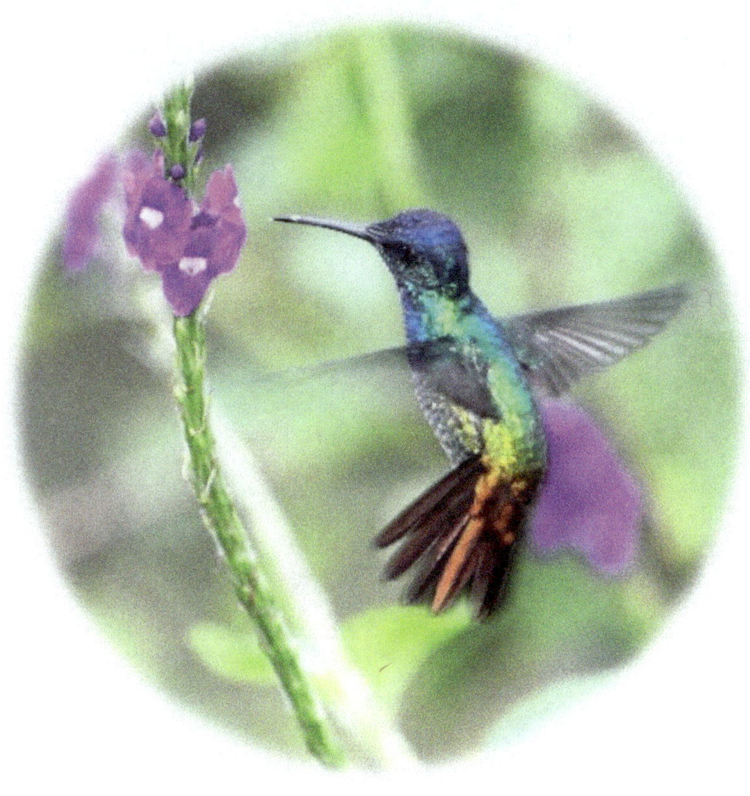

Psalm 119:142-144

Thy righteousness is an everlasting
righteousness, and thy law is the truth.
Trouble and anguish have taken hold
on me: yet thy commandments
are my delights.
The righteousness of thy testimonies is
everlasting: give me understanding,
and I shall live.

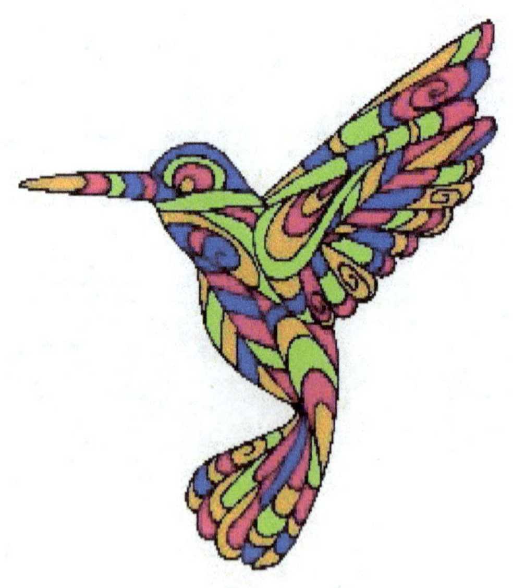

Psalm 119: 166-167

LORD, I have hoped for thy salvation,
and done thy commandments.
My soul hath kept thy testimonies;
and I love them exceedingly.

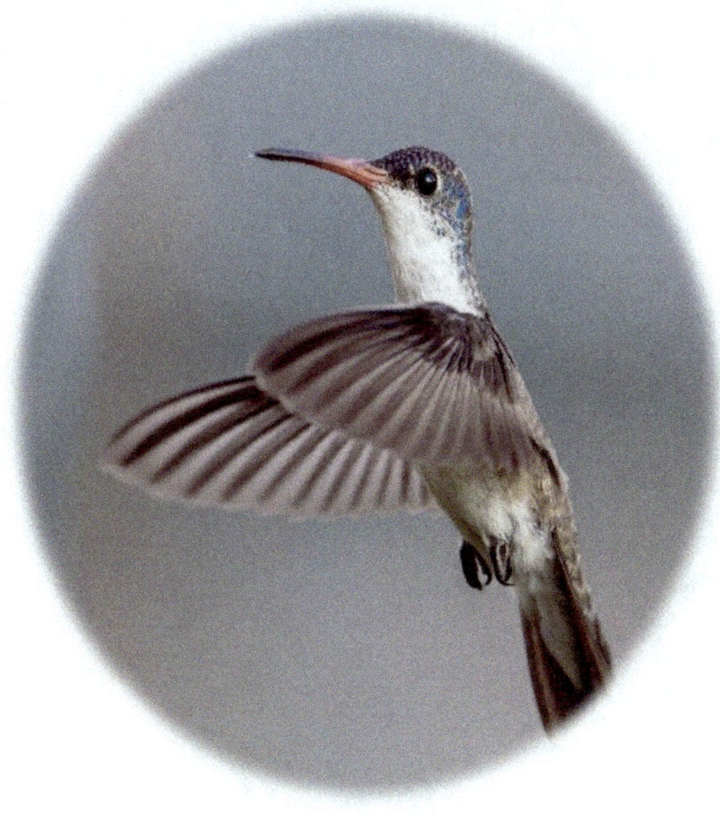

Psalm 146:5-6

Happy is he that hath the God of Jacob
for his help,
whose hope is in the LORD his God:
Which made heaven, and earth, the sea,
and all that therein is: which
keepeth truth forever:

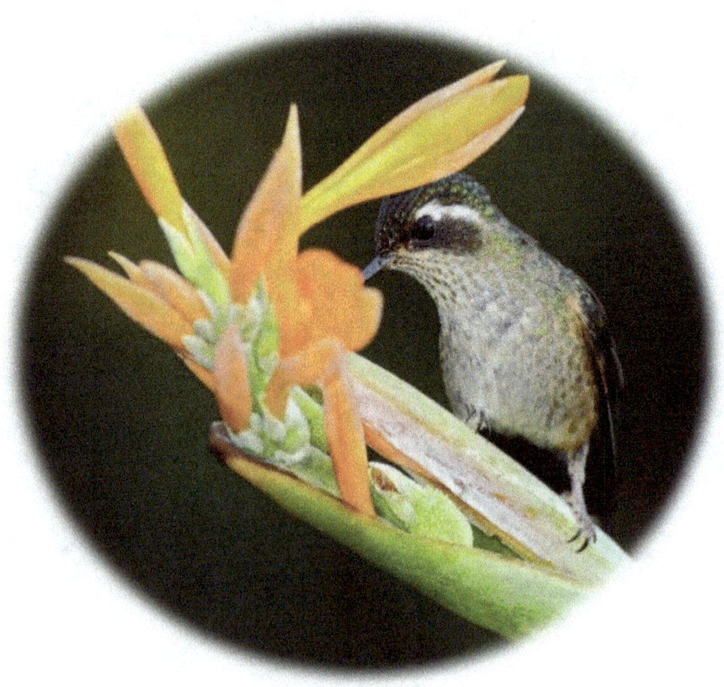

Proverbs 14:32

…the righteous hath hope in his death.

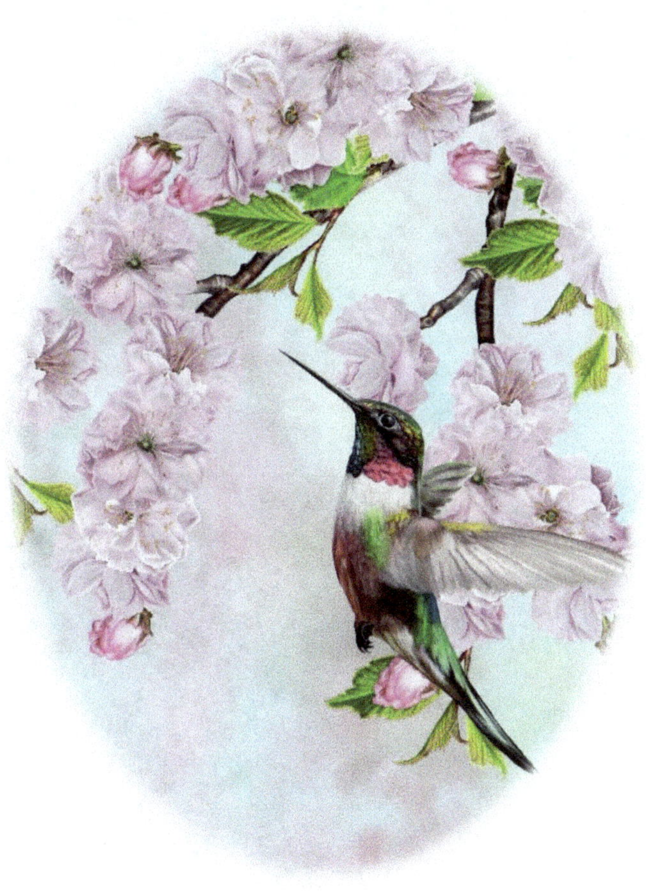

Proverbs 26:12

Seest thou a man wise in his own conceit? there is more hope of a fool than of him.

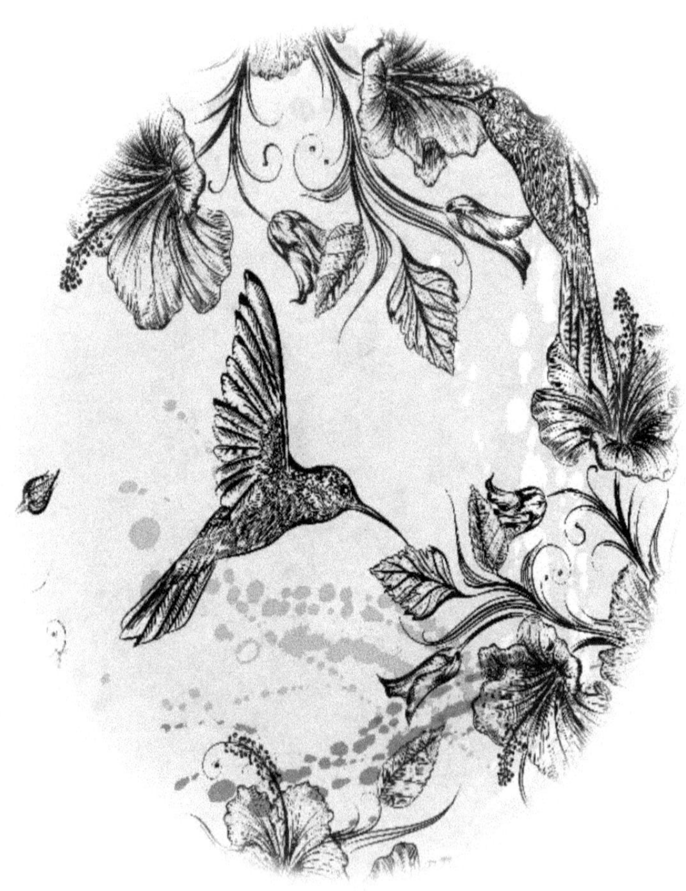

Jeremiah 17:17

Be not a terror unto me:
thou art my hope in the day of evil.

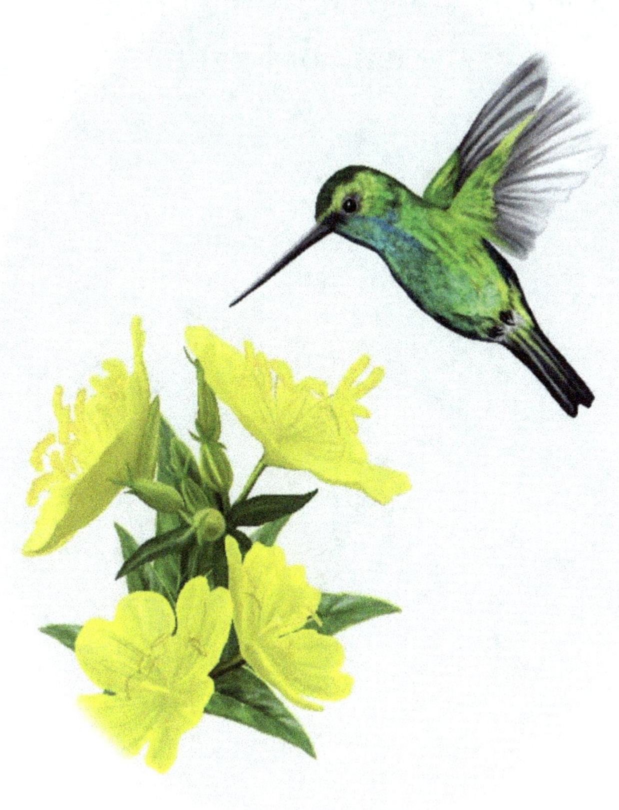

Hosea 2:15

And I will give her her vineyards from thence, and the valley of Achor for a door of hope: and she shall sing there, as in the days of her youth, and as in the day when she came up out of the land of Egypt.

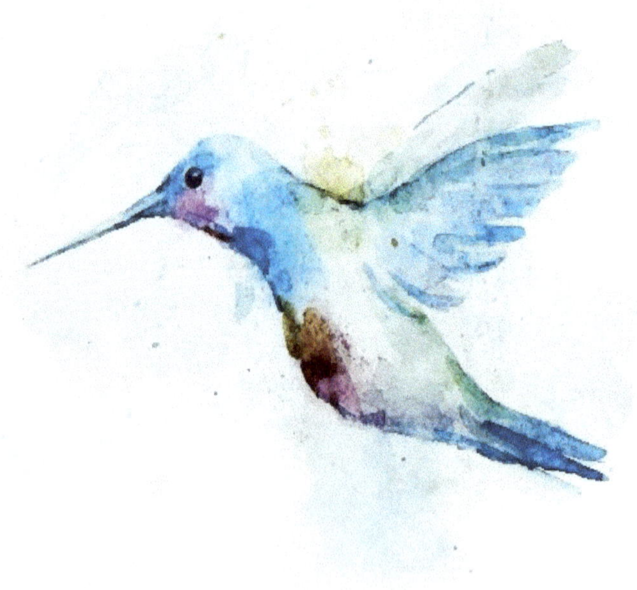

Job 8:5-7

But if you would earnestly seek God
and ask the Almighty for mercy,
If you are pure and upright, even now
He will rouse Himself on your behalf
and restore your righteous estate.
Though your beginnings were modest,
your latter days will flourish.

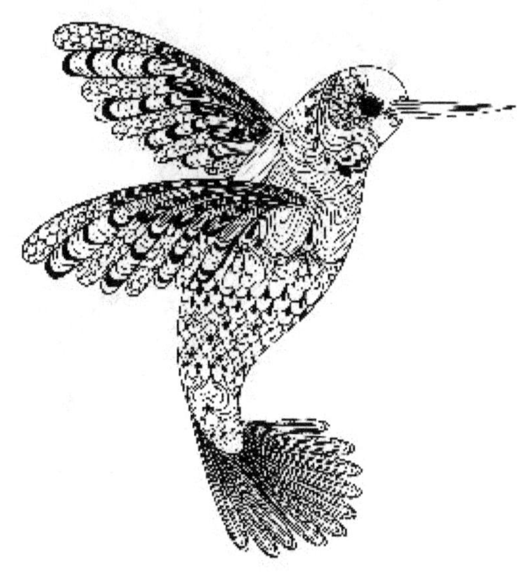

Job 17:15

And where is now my hope?
as for my hope, who shall see it?

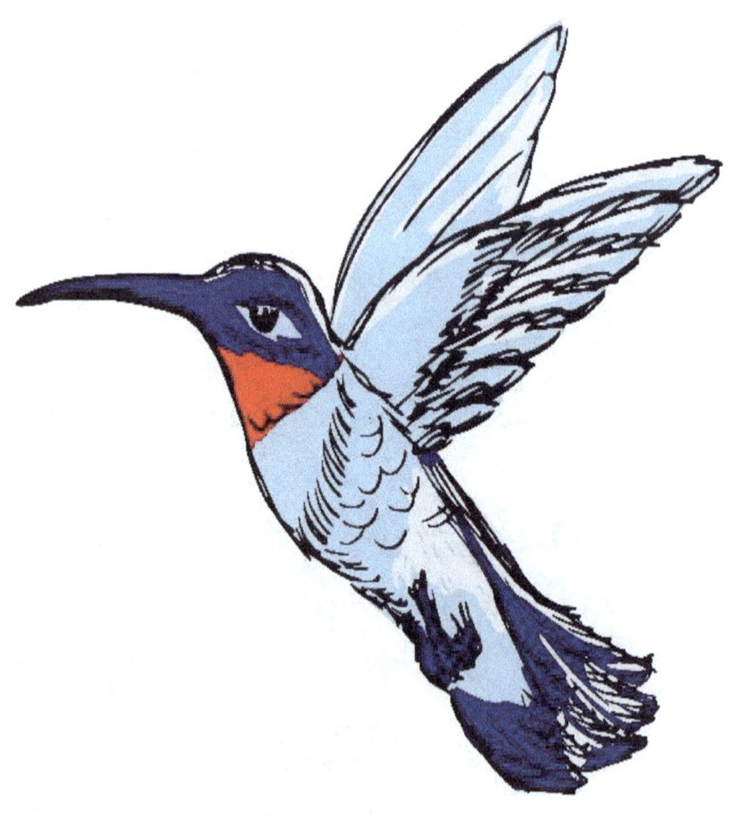

Job 27:8

For what is the hope of the hypocrite,
though he hath gained,
when God taketh away his soul?

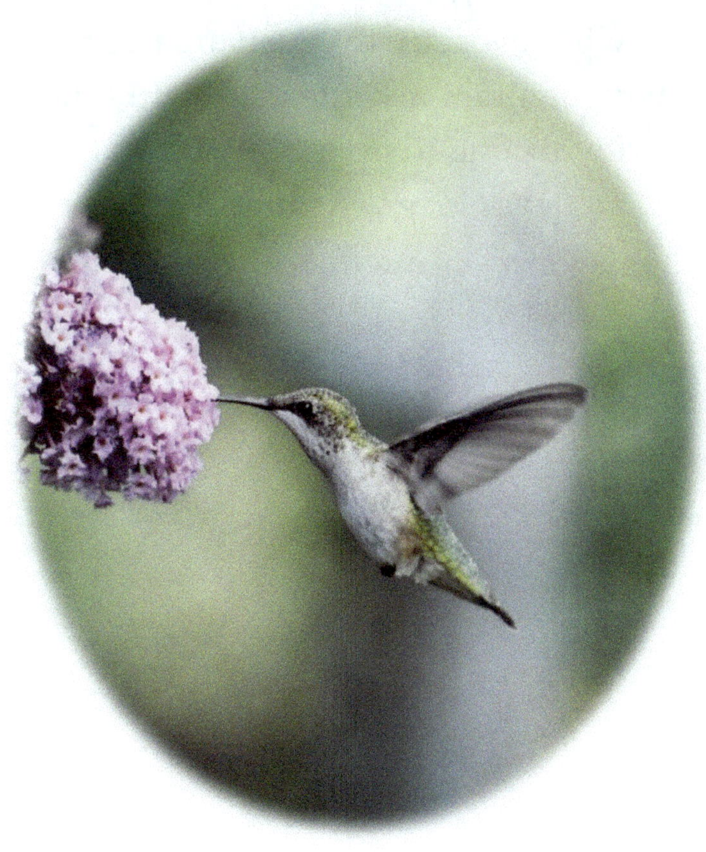

Job 27:2-6

As surely as God lives…as long as
my breath is still within me and
the breath of God remains in my nostrils,
my lips will not speak wickedness,
and my tongue will not utter deceit.
I will never say that you are right;
I will maintain my integrity until I die.
I will cling to my righteousness
and never let go. As long as I live,
my conscience will not accuse me.

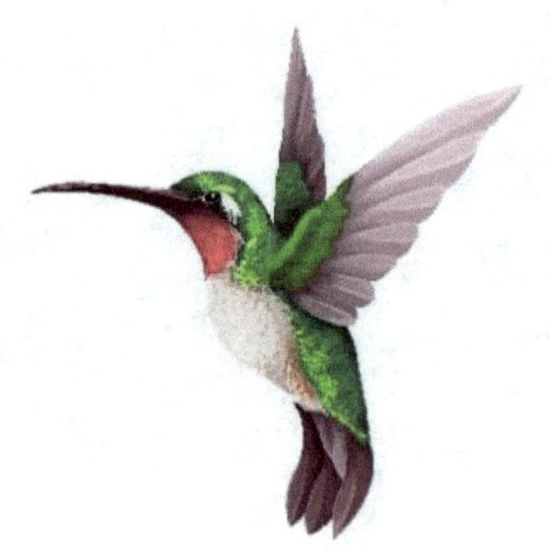

Lamentations 3:24

The LORD is my portion, saith my soul; therefore will I hope in him.

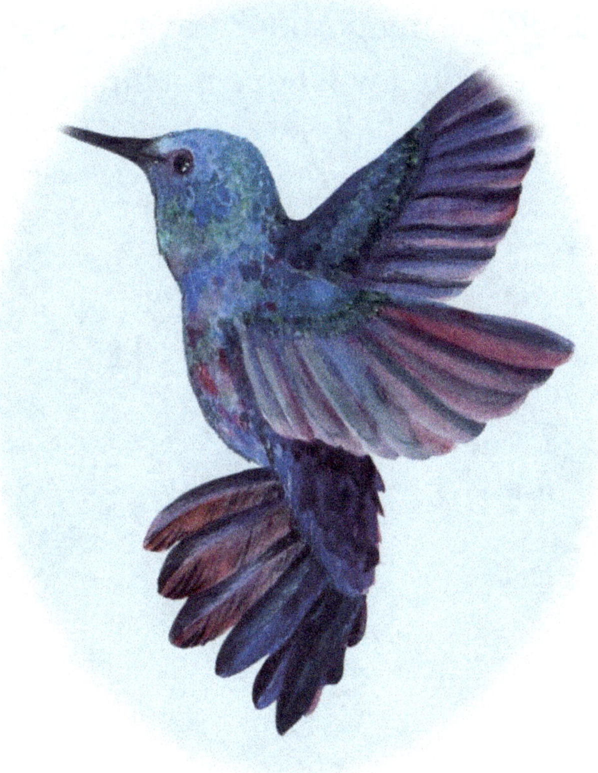

Lamentations 3:22-25

Because of the loving devotion
of the LORD we are not consumed,
for His mercies never fail.
They are new every morning;
great is Your faithfulness!
"The LORD is my portion," says my soul,
"Therefore I will hope in Him."

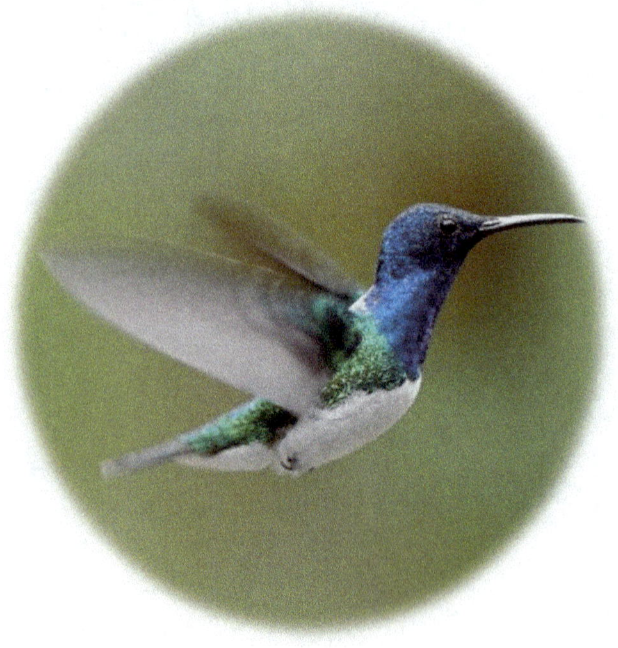

Lamentations 3:25-26

The LORD is good to those who wait
for Him, to the soul who seeks Him.
It is good to wait quietly
for the salvation of the LORD.

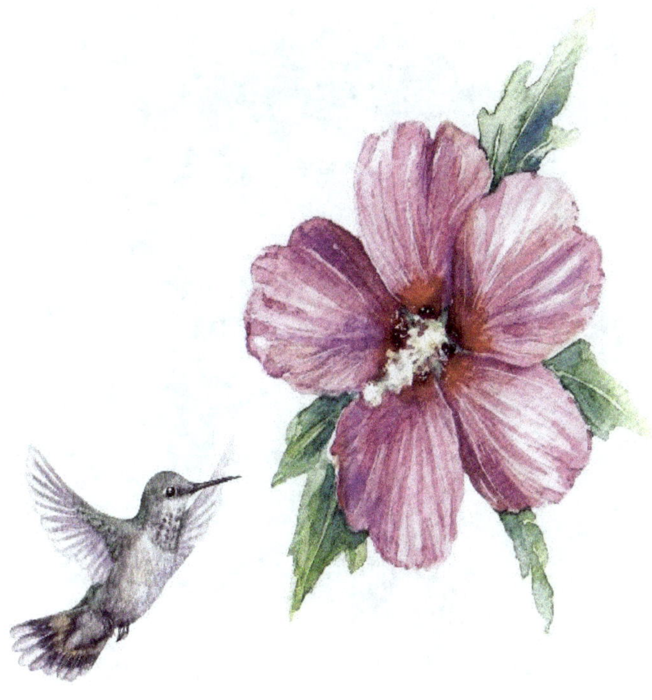

Lamentations 3: 57-58

You drew near when I called on You;
You said, "Do not be afraid."
You defend my cause, O Lord;
You redeem my life.

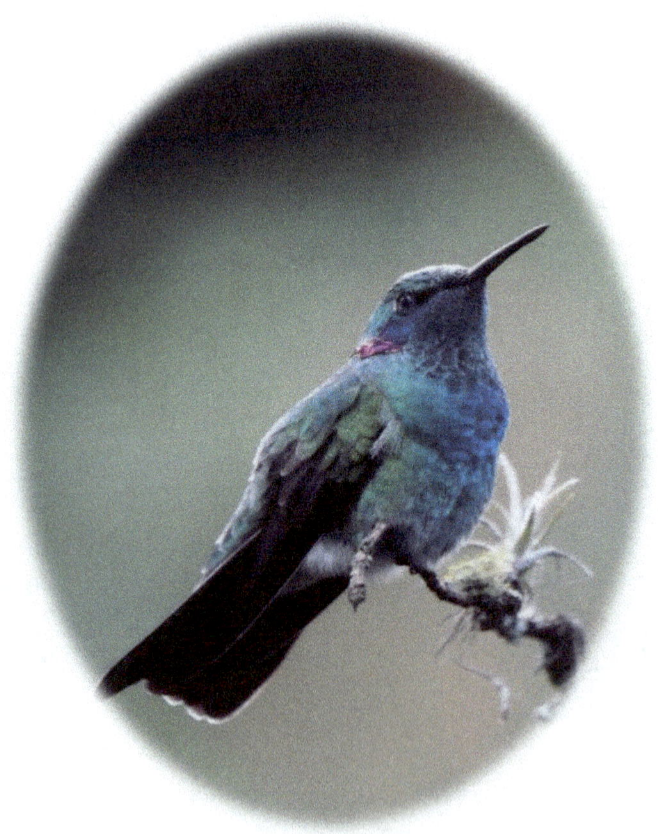

Act 2:26
Therefore did my heart rejoice,
and my tongue was glad;
moreover also my flesh
shall rest in hope:

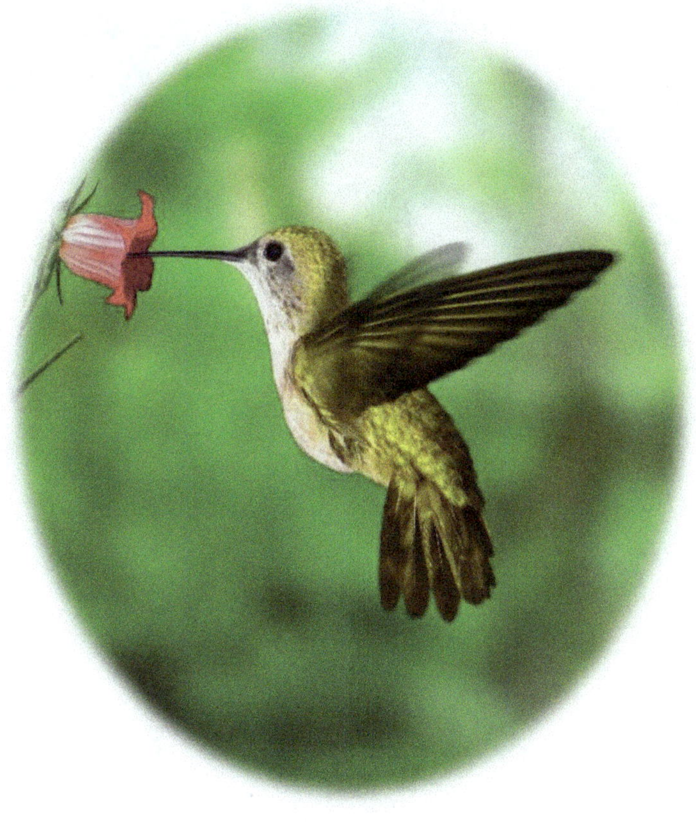

Acts 24:15

And have hope toward God,
which they themselves also allow,
that there shall be a resurrection
of the dead,
both of the just and unjust.

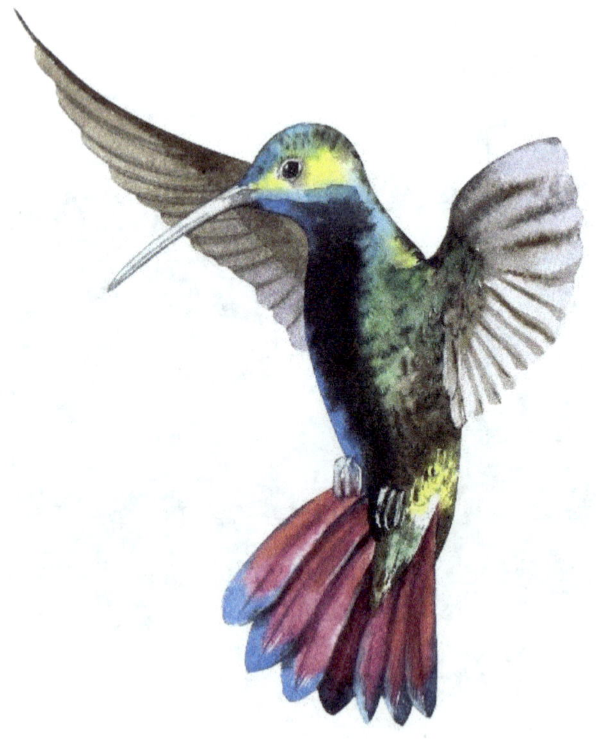

Romans 5:2

By whom also we have access by faith into this grace wherein we stand and rejoice in hope of the glory of God

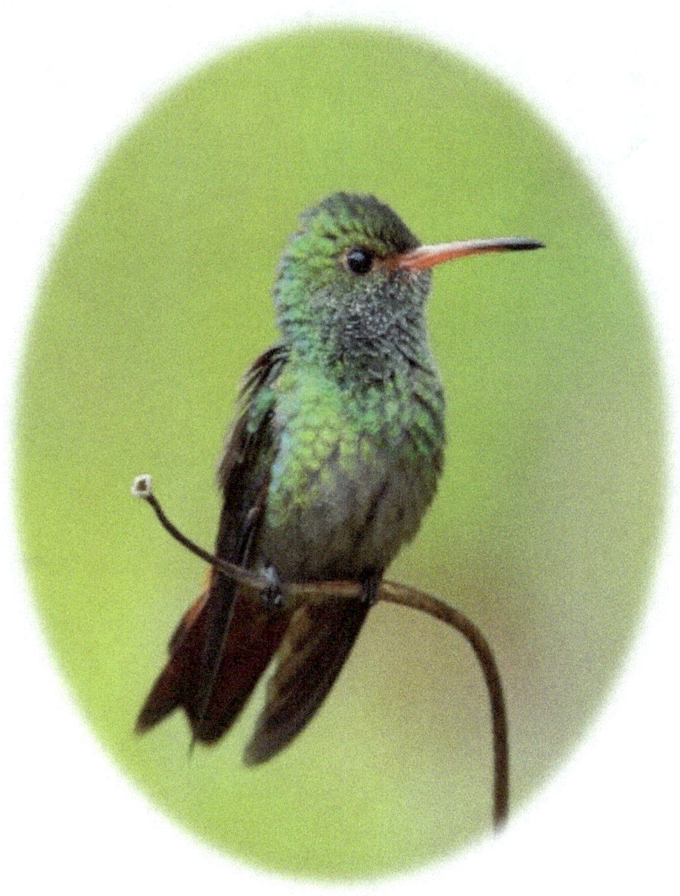

Psalm 33:18

Behold, the eye of the Lord is upon them
that fear him, upon them that hope
in his mercy

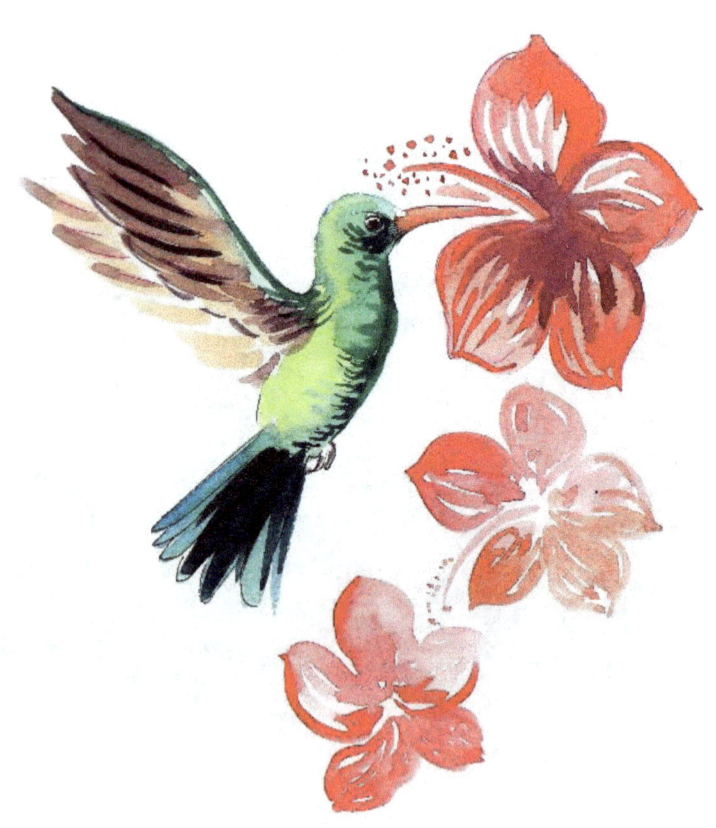

Psalm 33:20-22

Our soul waiteth for the Lord:
he is our help and our shield.
For our heart shall rejoice in him,
because we have trusted in his holy name.
Let thy mercy, O Lord, be upon us,
according as we hope in thee.

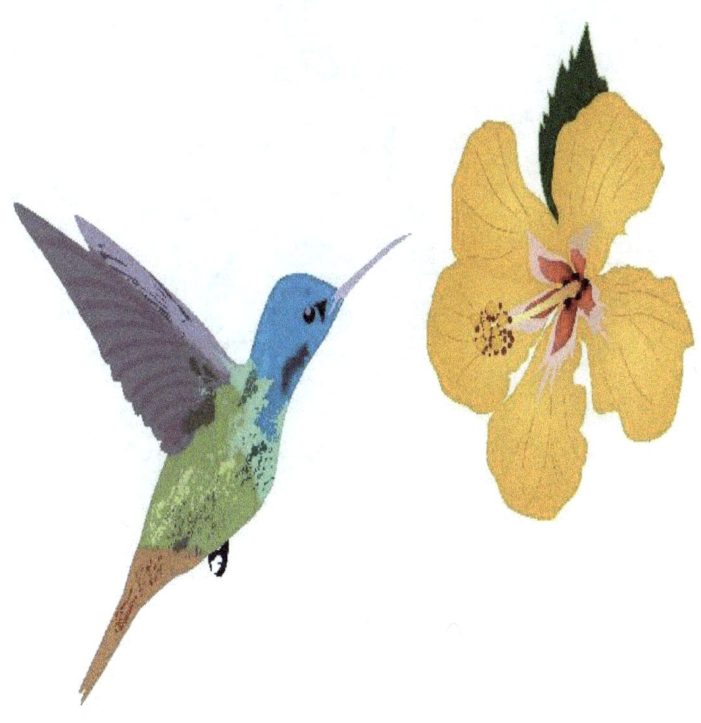

Proverbs 10:28

The hope of the righteous
shall be gladness…

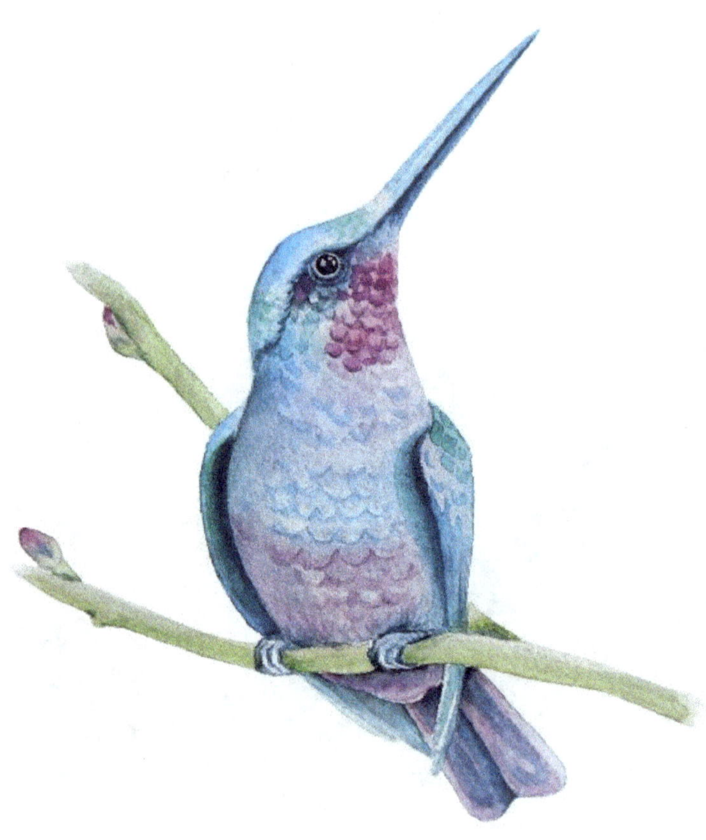

Psalm 42:5

Why art thou cast down, O my soul? and why art thou disquieted in me? hope thou in God: for I shall yet praise him for the help of his countenance.

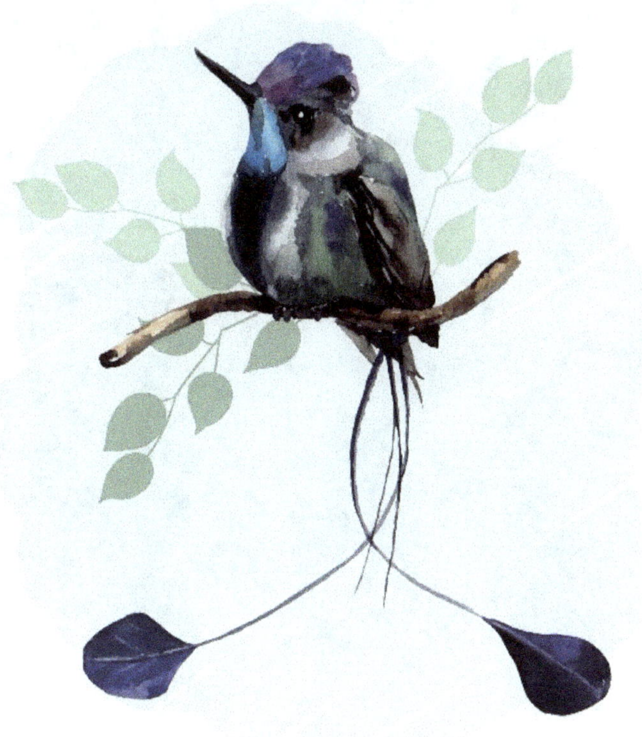

Psalm 147:11

The LORD taketh pleasure in them that fear him, in those that hope in his mercy.

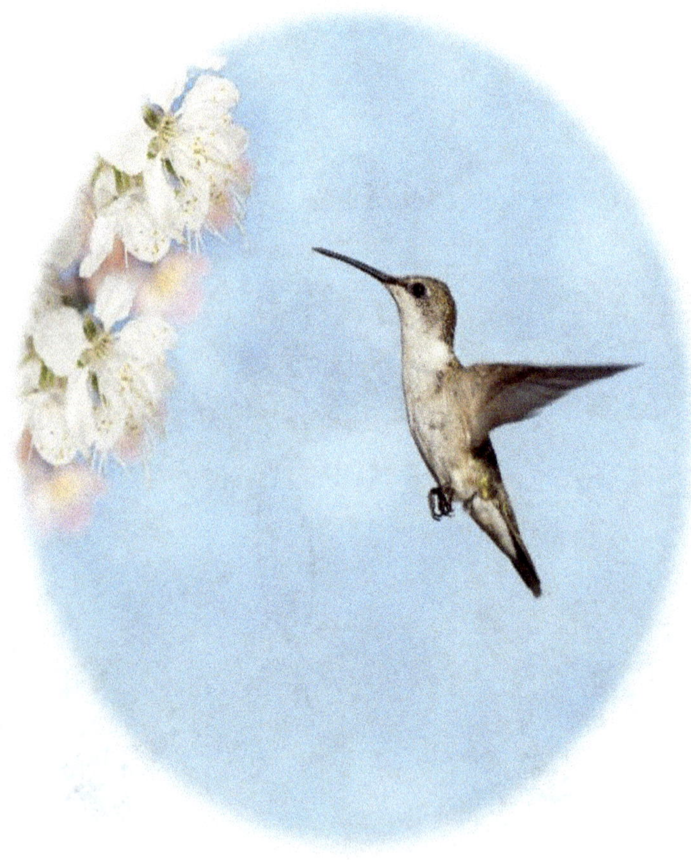

Psalm 130:5

I wait for the LORD, my soul doth wait,
and in his word do I hope.

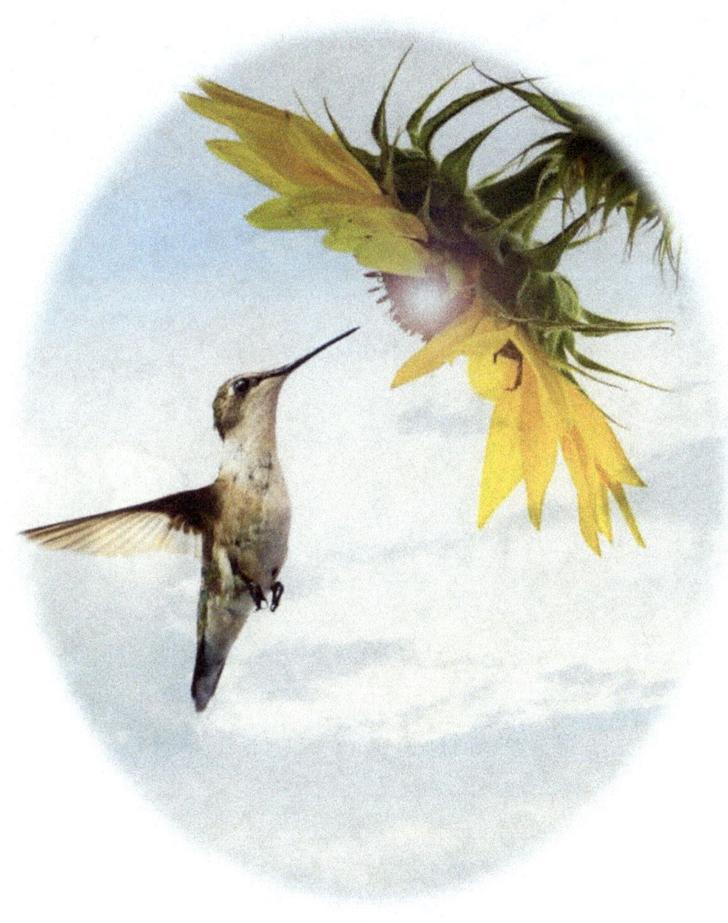

Psalm 130: 7

Let Israel hope in the Lord:
for with the Lord there is mercy,
and with him is plenteous redemption.

Jeremiah 17:7

Blessed is the man that trusteth
in the LORD,
and whose hope the LORD is.

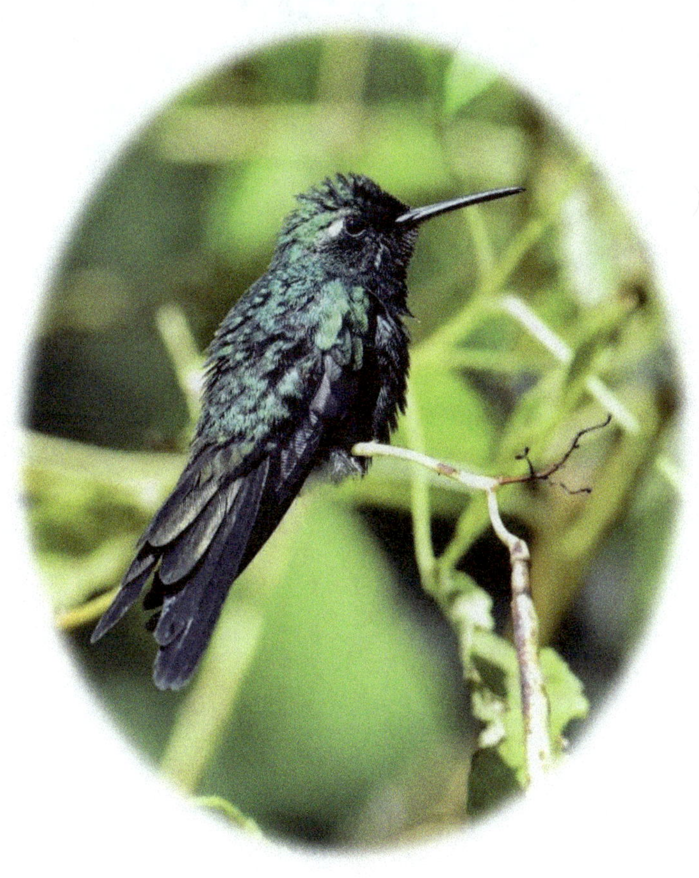

Hebrews 6:19

Which hope we have as an anchor of the soul, both sure and stedfast, and which entereth into that within the veil.

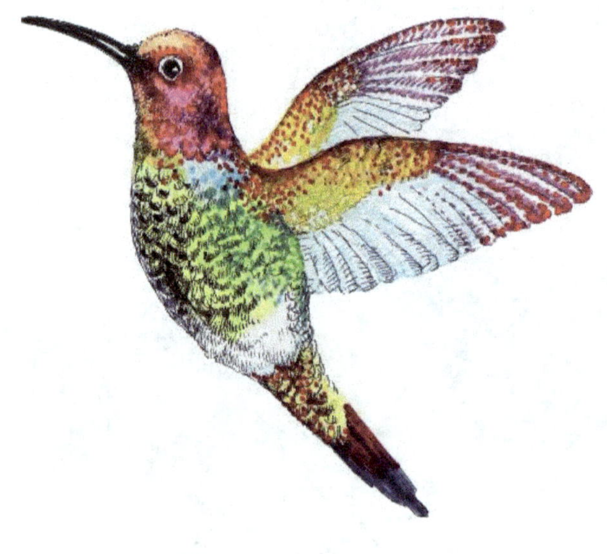

Ephesians 4:4

There is one body, and one Spirit, even as ye are called in one hope of your calling.

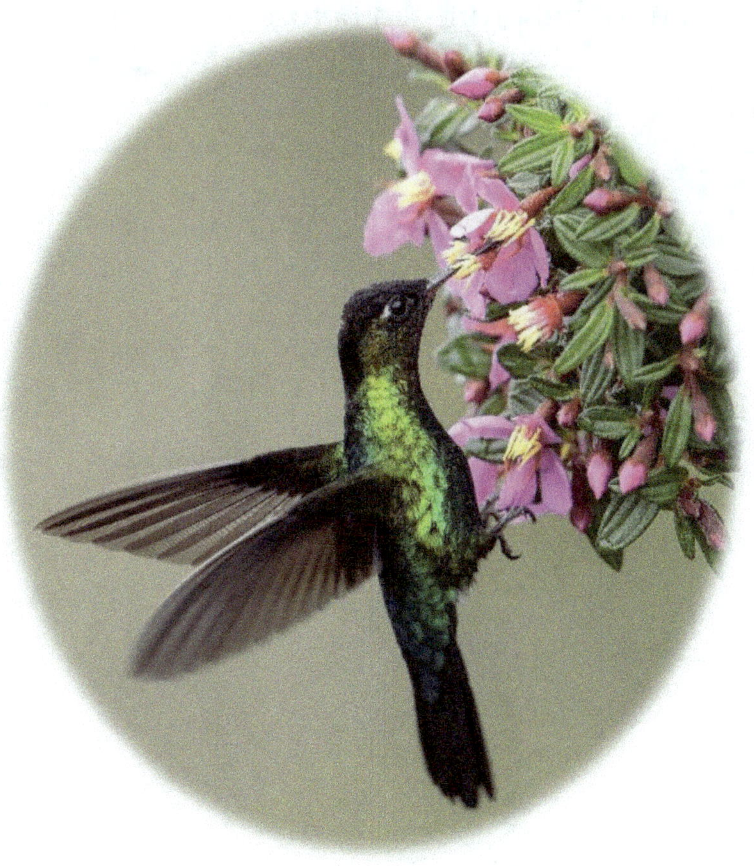

Titus 1:2

In hope of eternal life, which God, that cannot lie, promised before the world began.

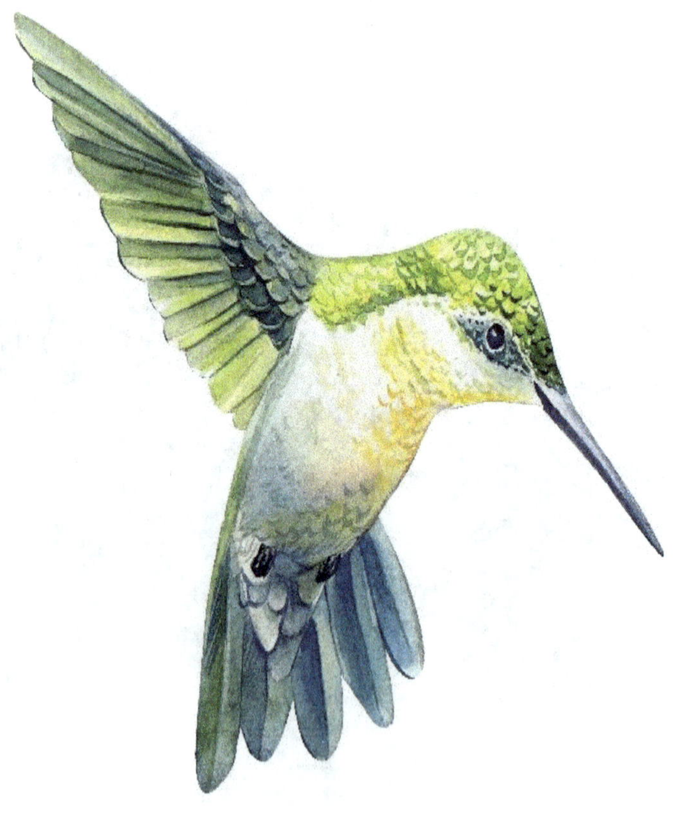

Romans 10:11

For the scripture saith, Whosoever believeth on him shall not be ashamed.

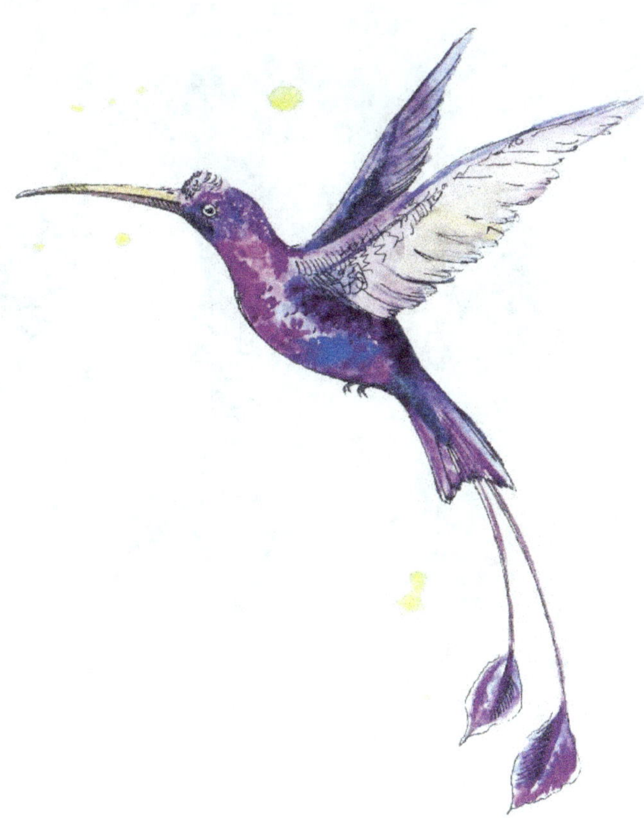

1 Corinthians 2:5

That your faith should not stand in the wisdom of men, but in the power of God.

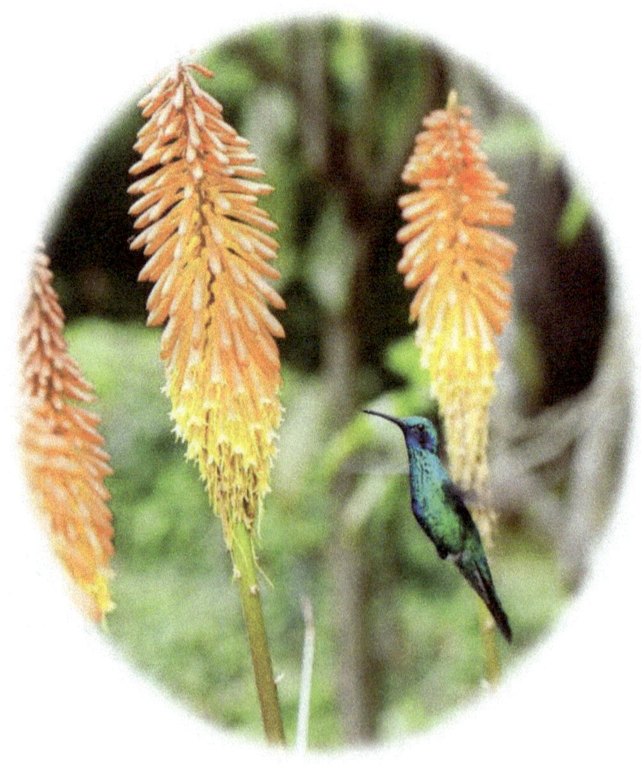

Psalm 25:5

Guide me in your truth and teach me, for you are God my Savior, and my hope is in you all day long.

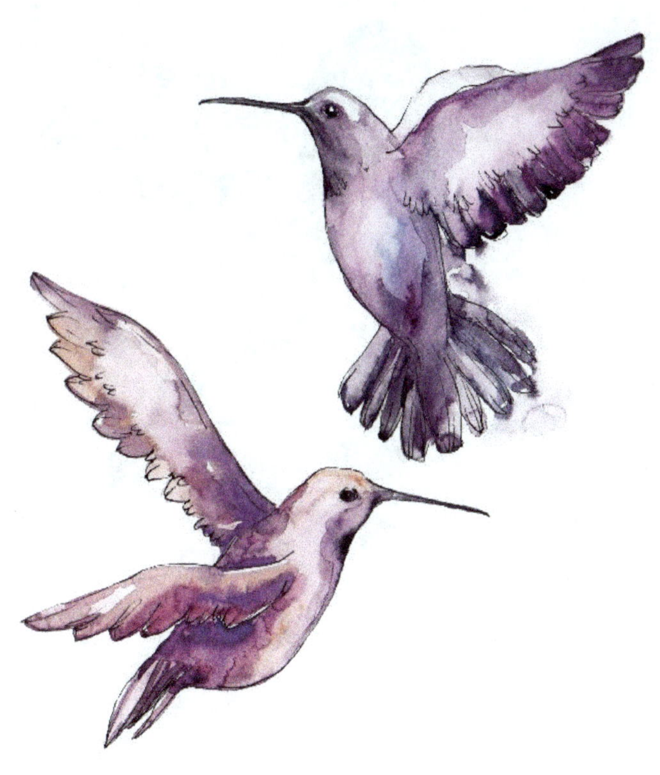

Psalm 34:18

The Lord is close to the brokenhearted and saves those who are crushed in spirit.

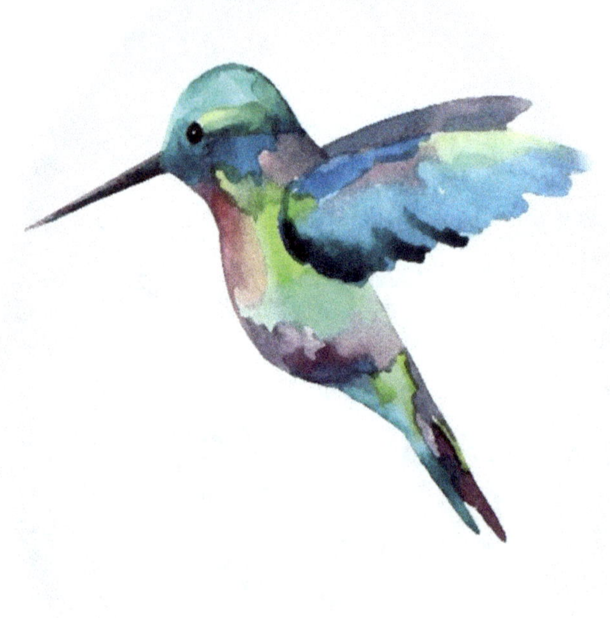

Psalm 55:22

Cast thy burden upon the Lord, and he shall sustain thee: he shall never suffer the righteous to be moved.

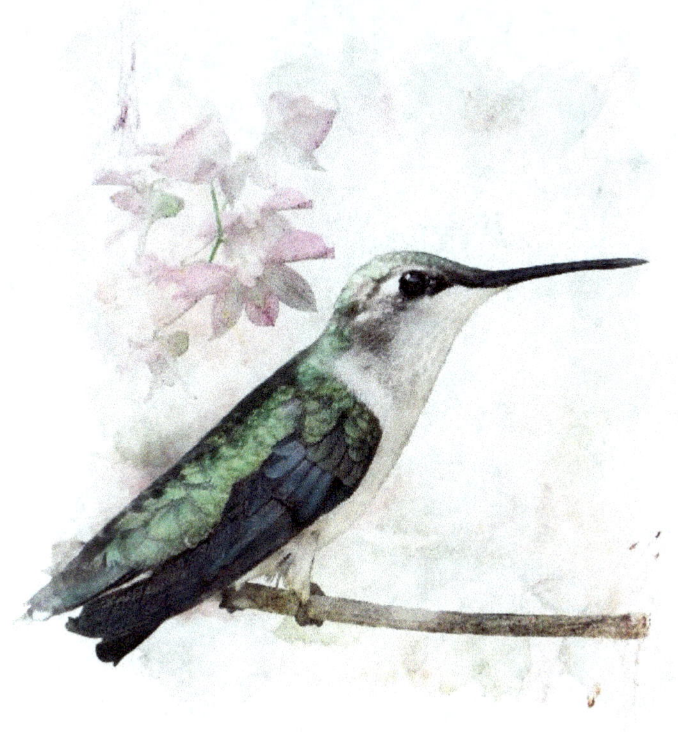

Romans 8:25

But if we hope for what we do not see, we eagerly wait for it with patience.

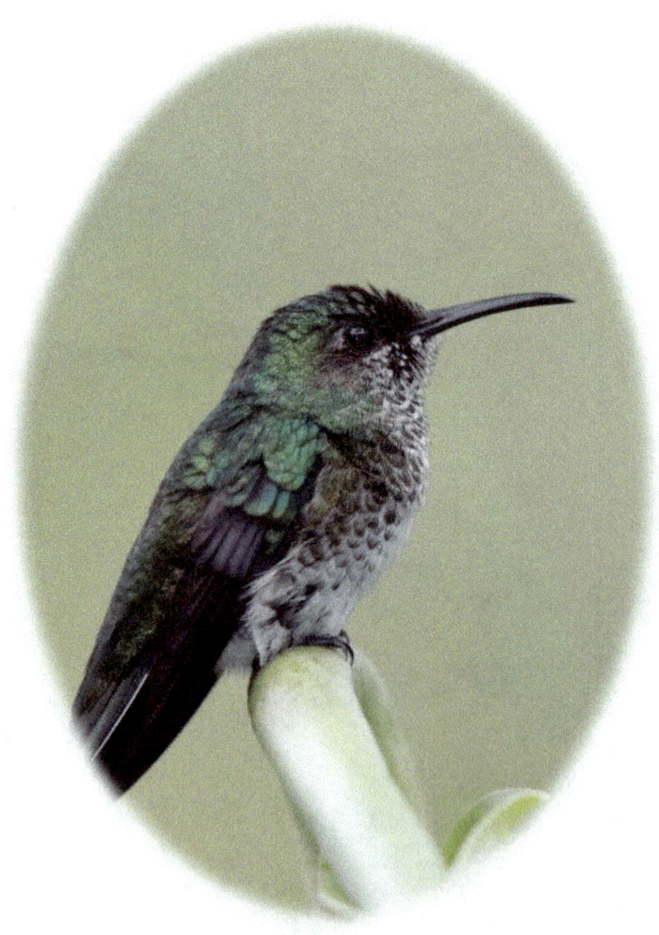

Romans 15:13

May the God of hope fill you with all joy and peace as you trust in him so that you may overflow with hope by the power of the Holy Spirit.

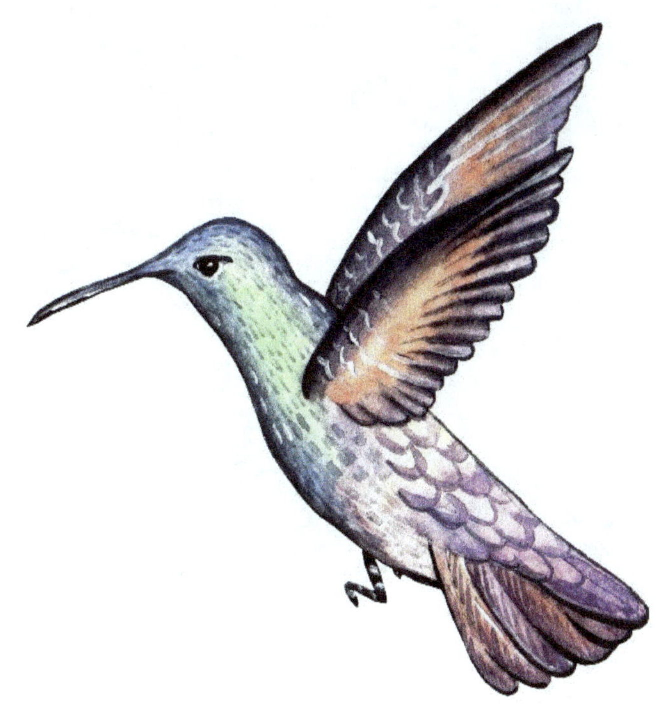

Romans 5:5

And hope does not disappoint us, because God has poured out his love into our hearts through the Holy Spirit, whom he has given us.

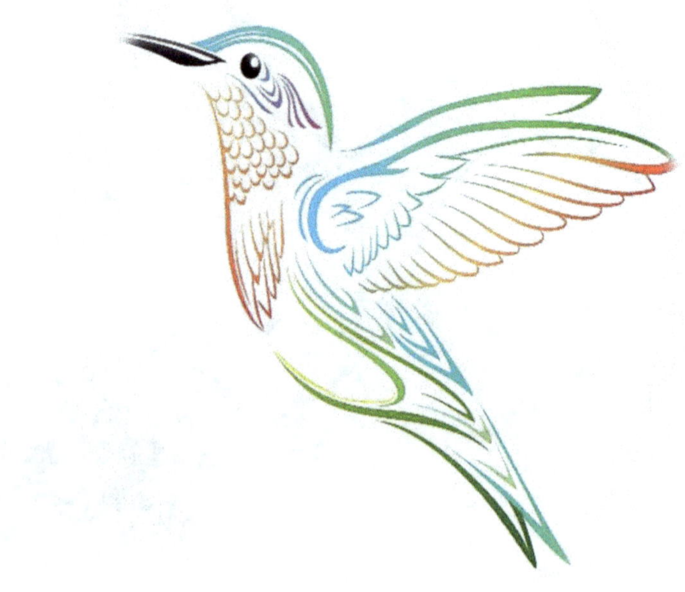

Hebrews 10:36

For ye have need of patience, that, after ye have done the will of God, ye might receive the promise.

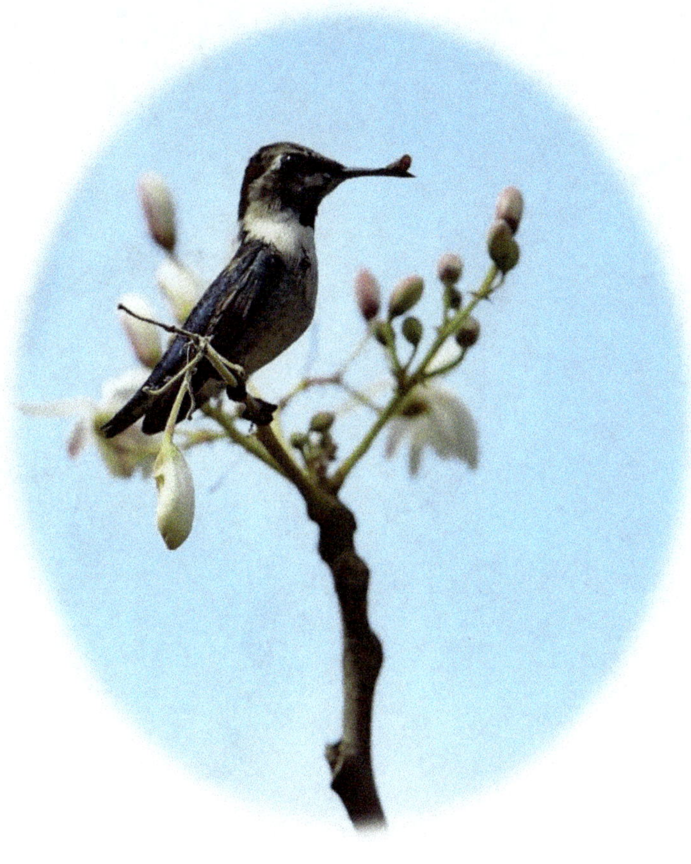

Romans 8:24

For we were saved in this hope, but hope that is seen is not hope; for why does one still hope for what he sees?

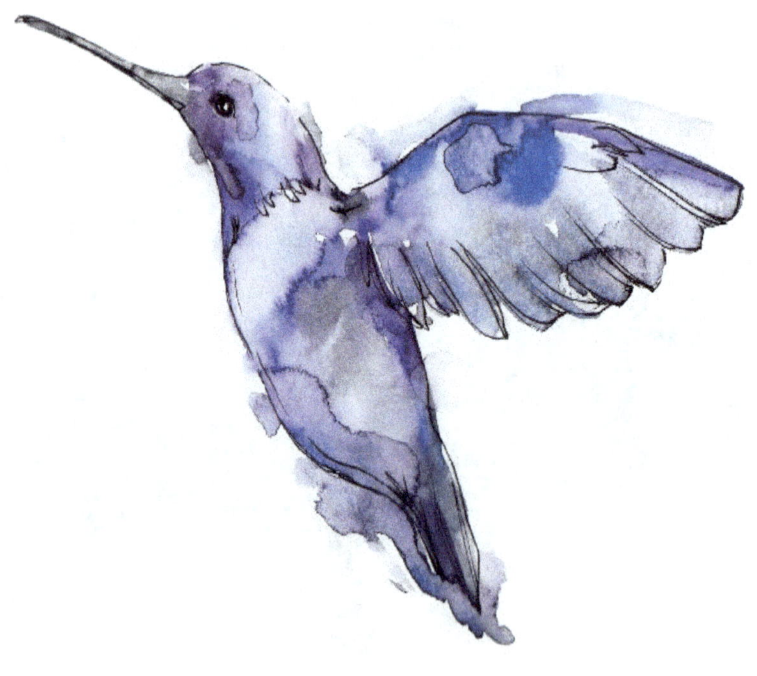

Romans 5:3-4

And not only so, but we glory in tribulations also: knowing that tribulation worketh patience; And patience, experience; and experience, hope.

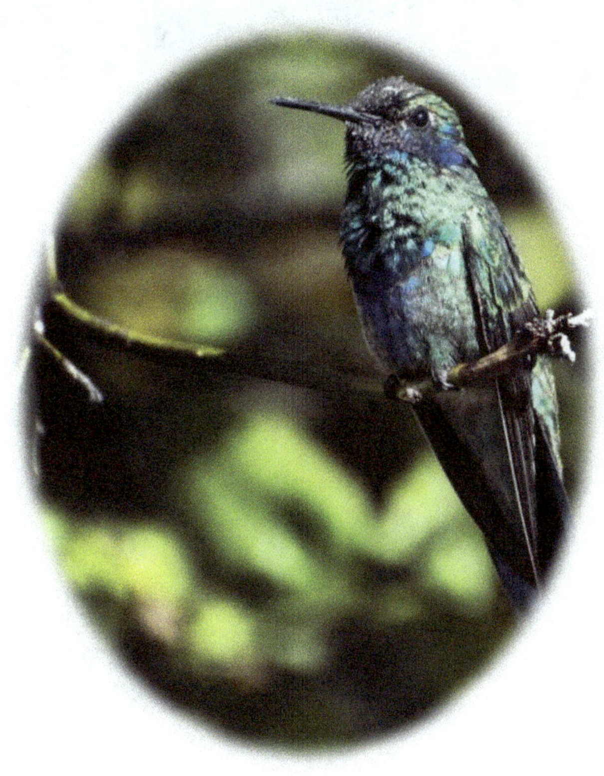

Galatians 6:9

And let us not be weary in well doing: for in due season we shall reap, if we faint not.

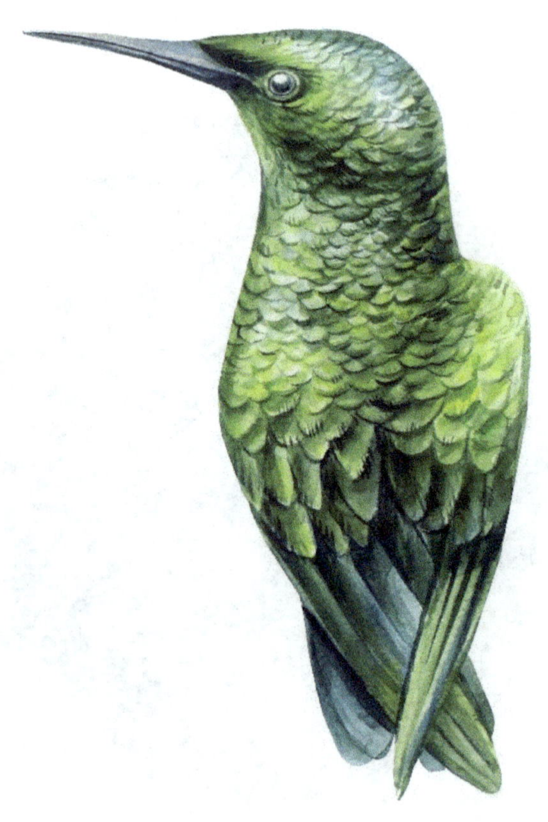

Romans 8:28

And we know that all things work together for good to them that love God, to them who are the called according to his purpose.

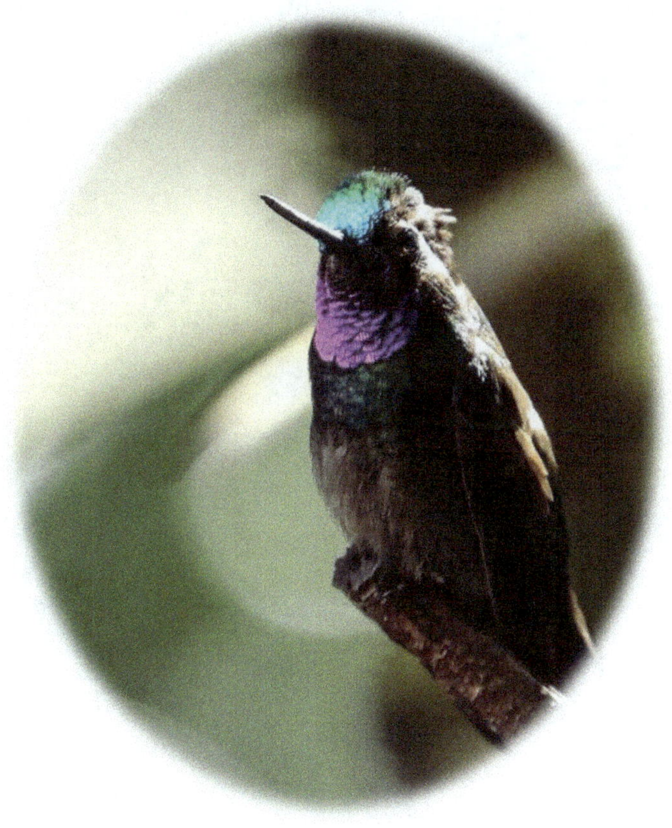

1 Thessalonians 5:11

Wherefore comfort yourselves together, and edify one another, even as also ye do.

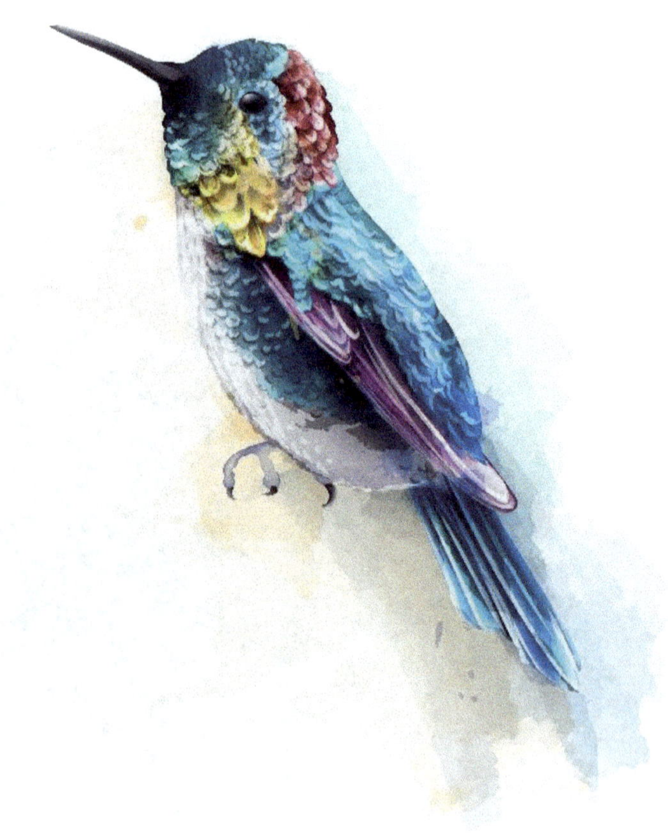

Deuteronomy 31:6

Be strong and of a good courage, fear not, nor be afraid of them: for the Lord thy God, he it is that doth go with thee; he will not fail thee, nor forsake thee.

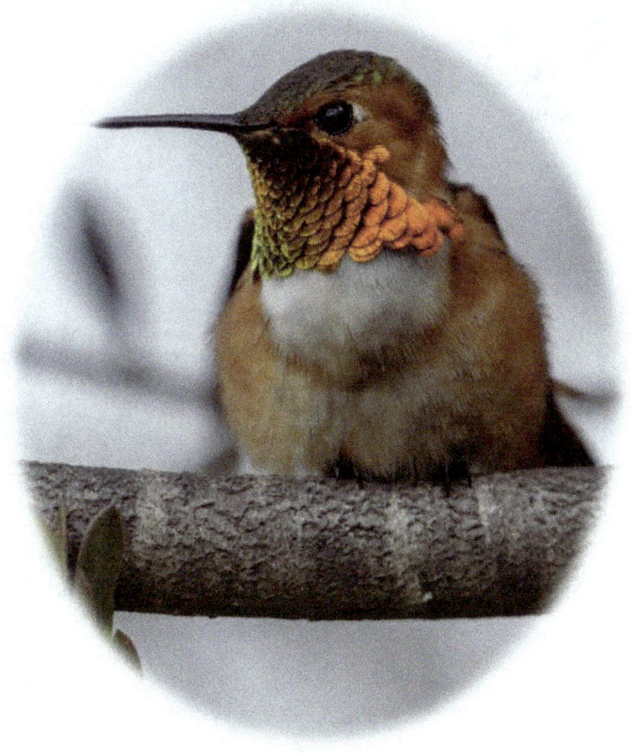

2 Chronicles 15:7

But as for you, be strong and do not give up, for your work will be rewarded.

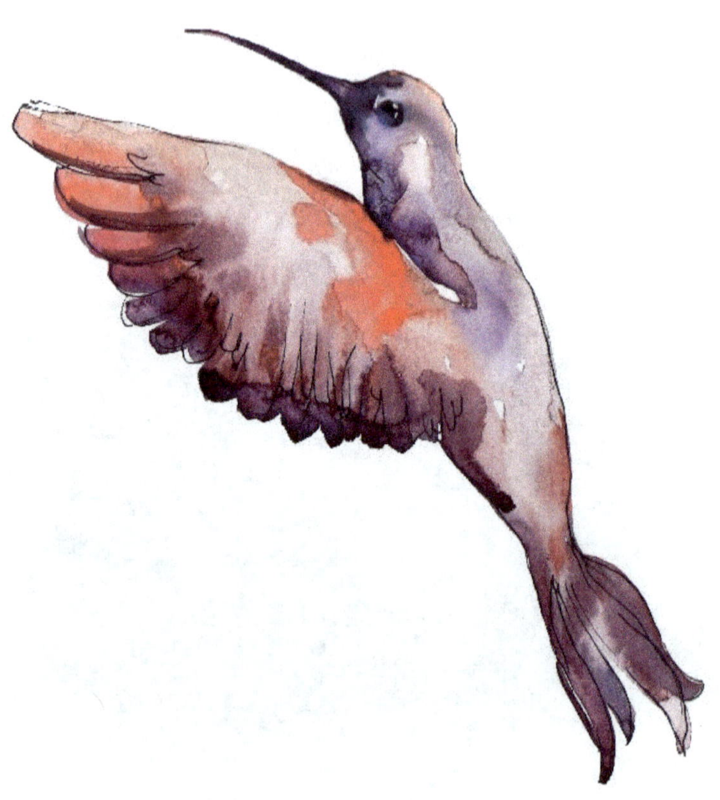

1 Peter 5:7

Cast all your anxiety on him because he cares for you.

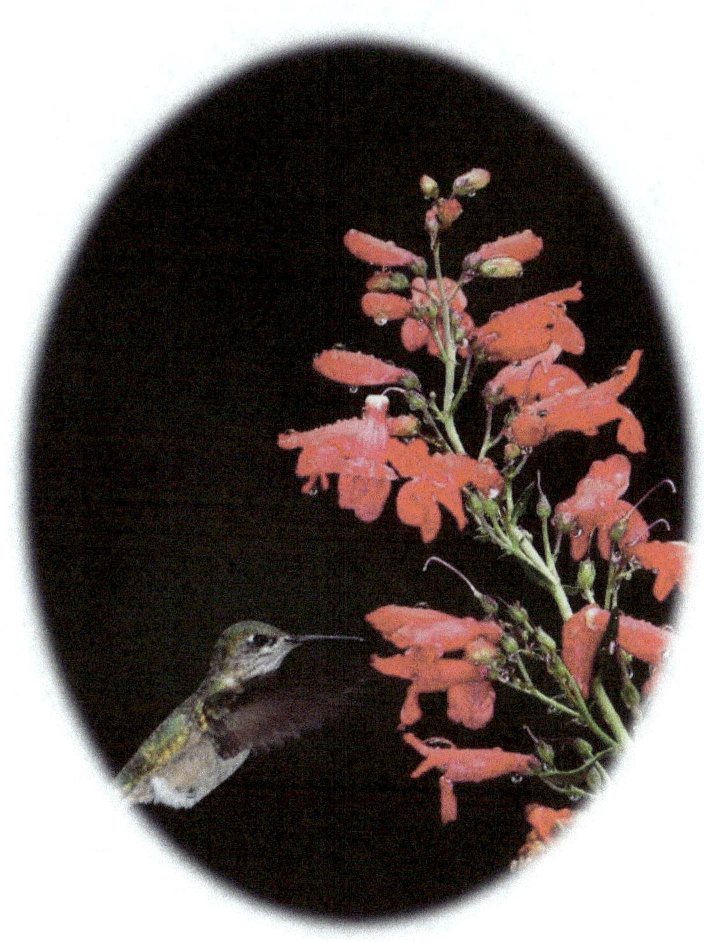

2 Corinthians 3:12

Therefore, since we have such a hope,
we are very bold.

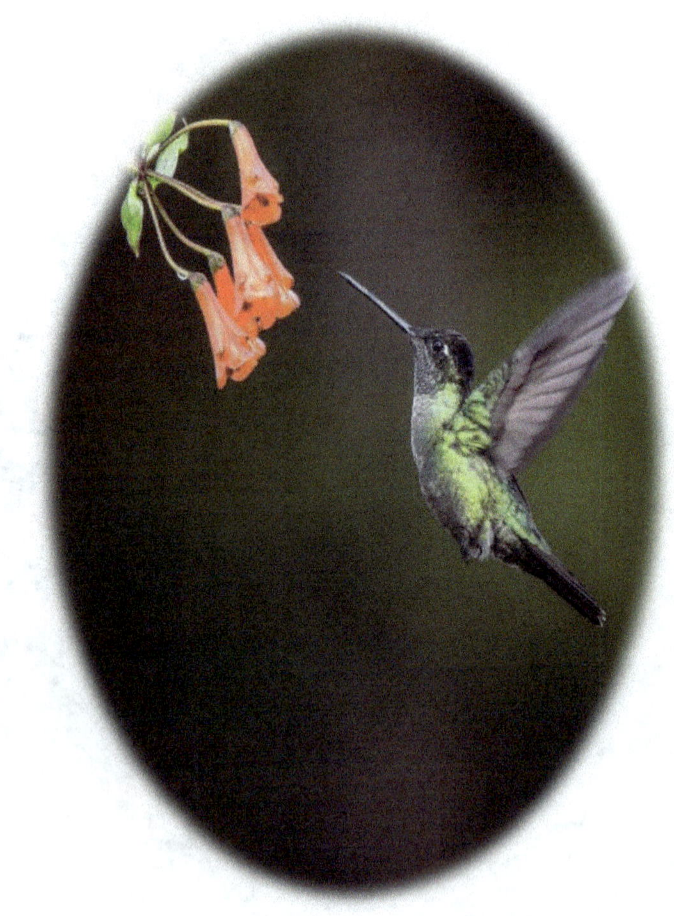

Hebrews 10:23

Let us hold unswervingly to the hope we profess, for he who promised is faithful.

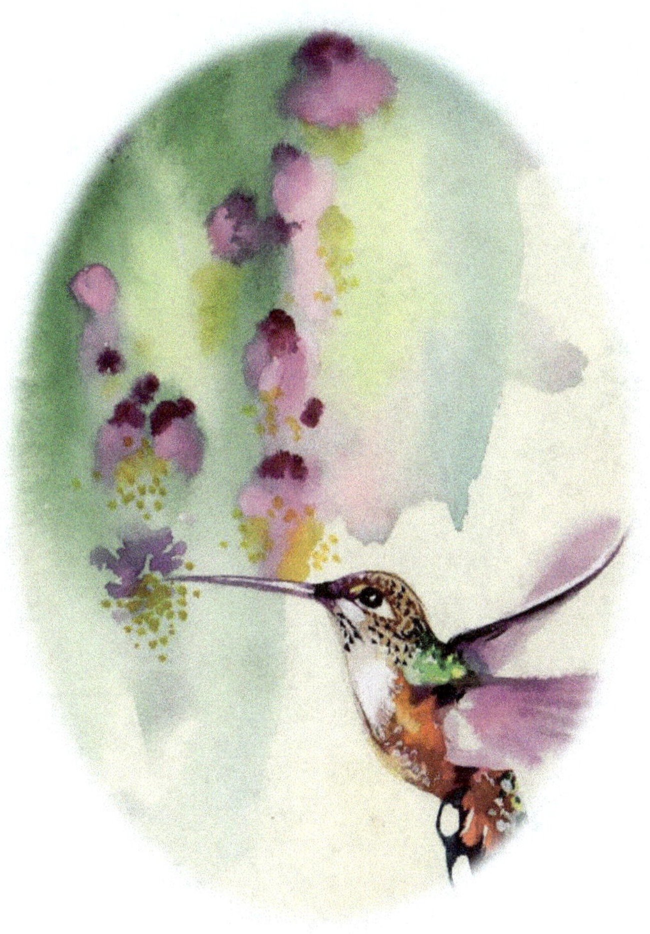

1 Corinthians 13:13

And now abideth faith, hope, charity, these three; but the greatest of these is charity.

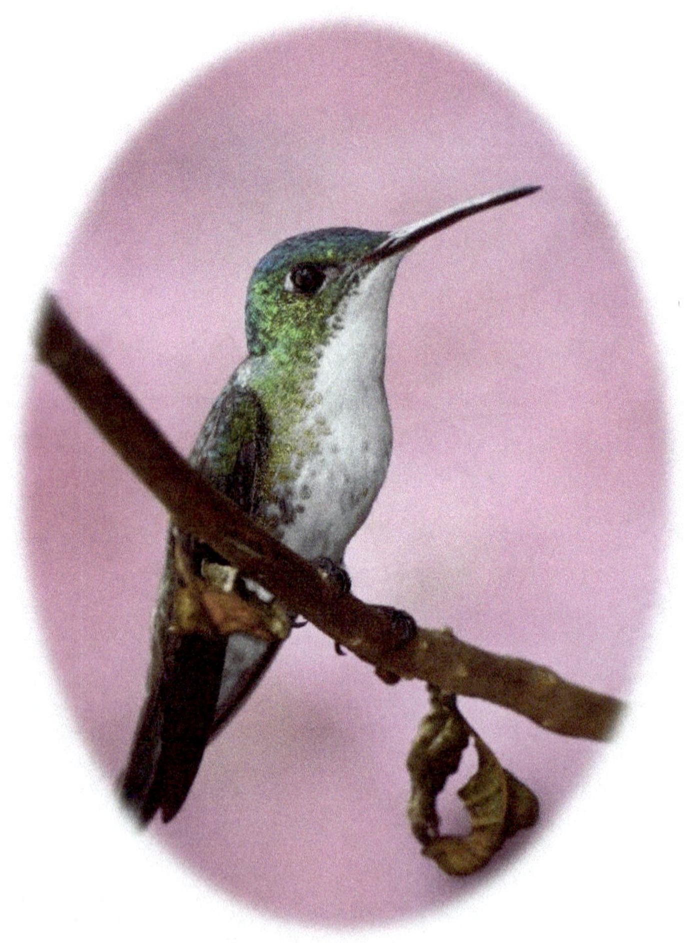

2 Timothy 1:7

For God hath not given us the spirit of fear; but of power, and of love, and of a sound mind.

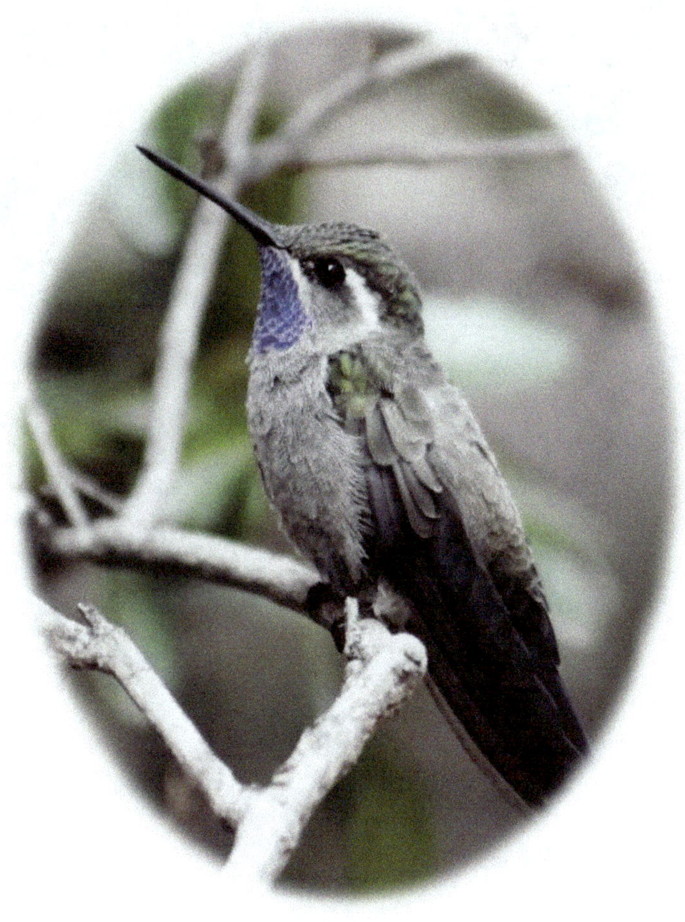

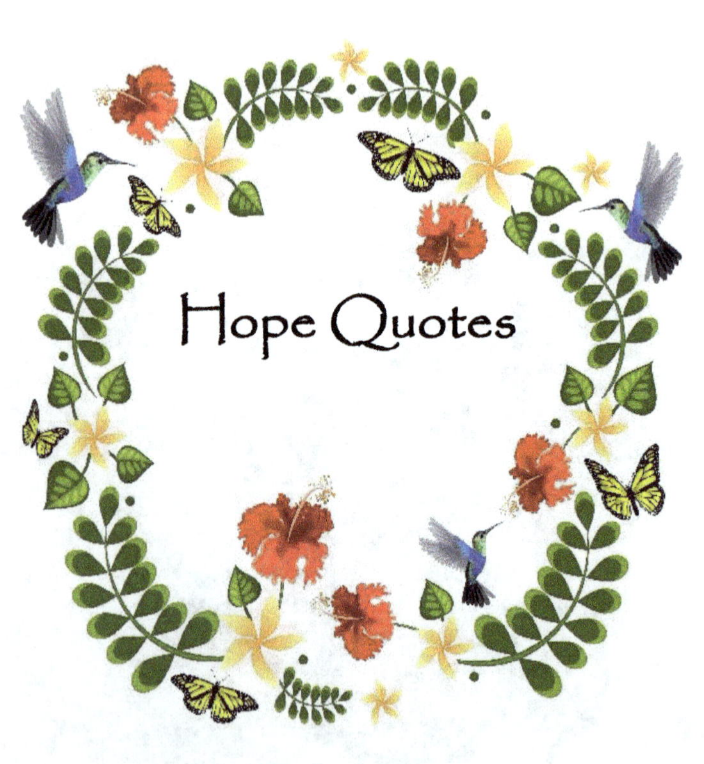

Hope Quotes

Hope can be a powerful force. Maybe there's no actual magic in it, but when you know what you hope for most and hold it like a light within you, you can make things happen, almost like magic.

Laini Taylor

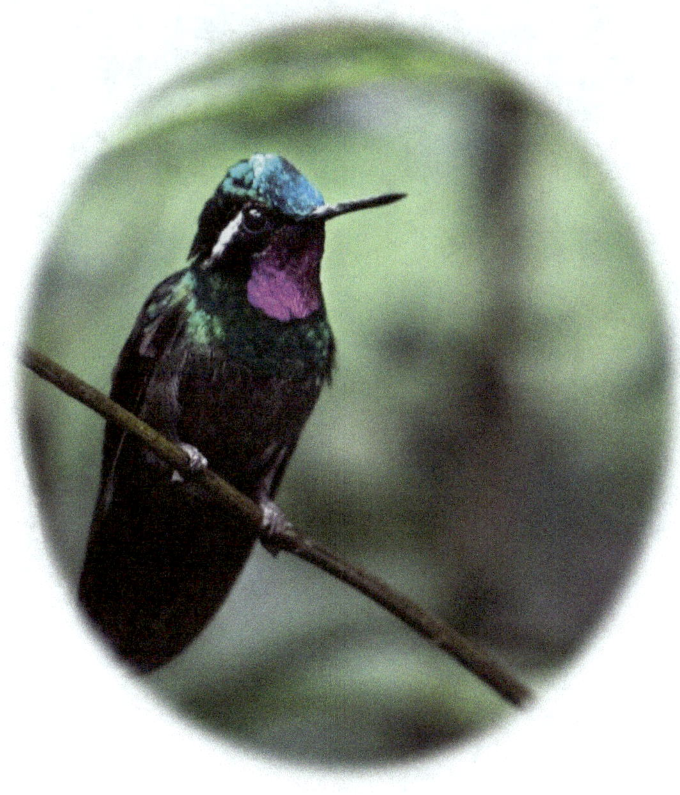

The road that is built in hope is more pleasant to the traveler than the road built in despair, even though they both lead to the same destination.

Marian Zimmer Bradley

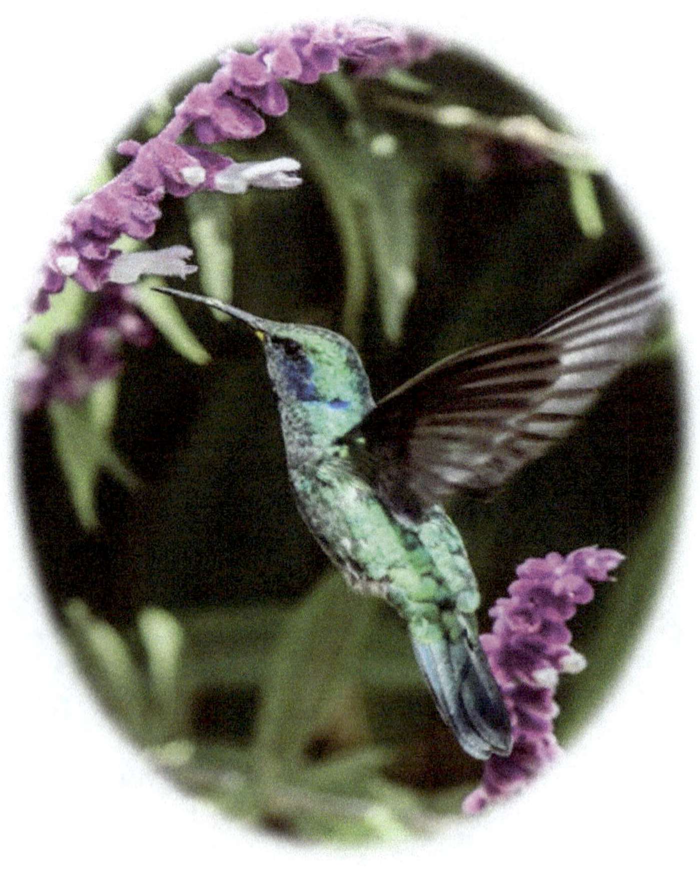

Hope is being able to see that there is light despite all of the darkness.

Desmond Tutu

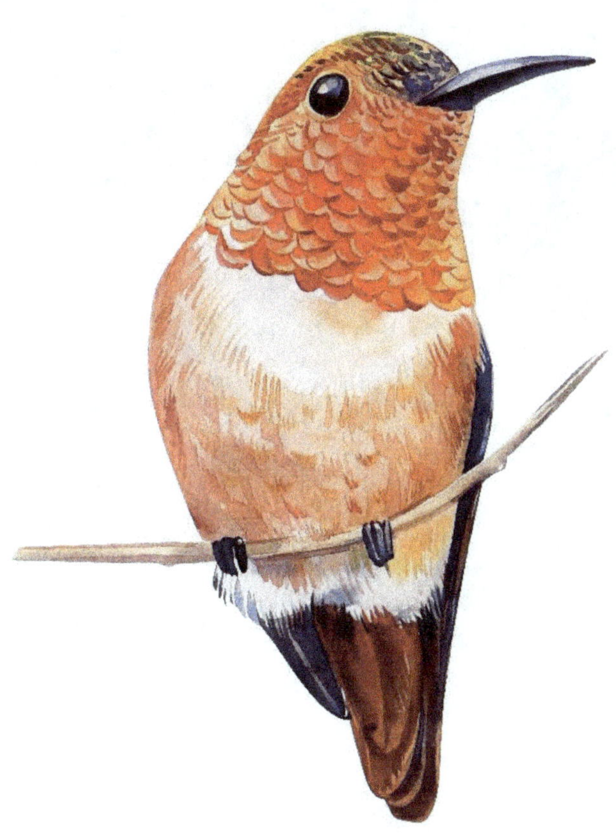

To live without hope is to cease
to live.

Fyodor Dostoevsky

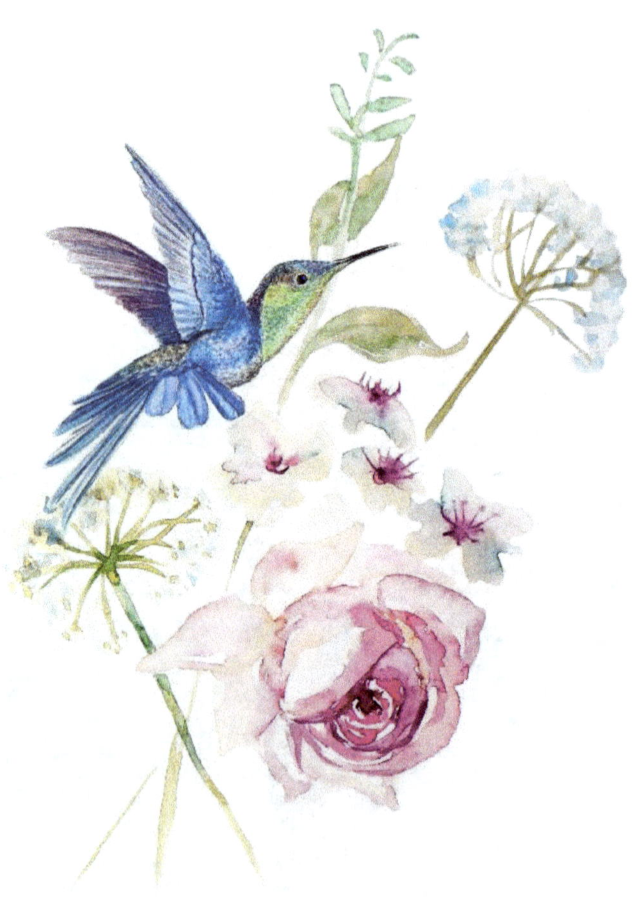

Hope is the companion of power, and the mother of success; for who so hopes strongly has within him the gift of miracles.

Samuel Smiles

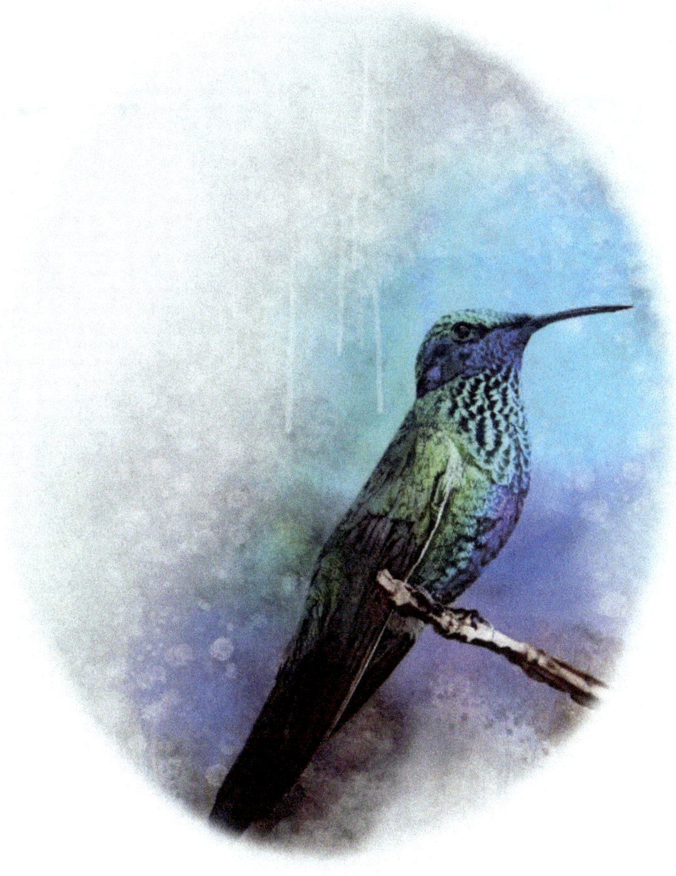

Hope is a waking dream.
Aristotle

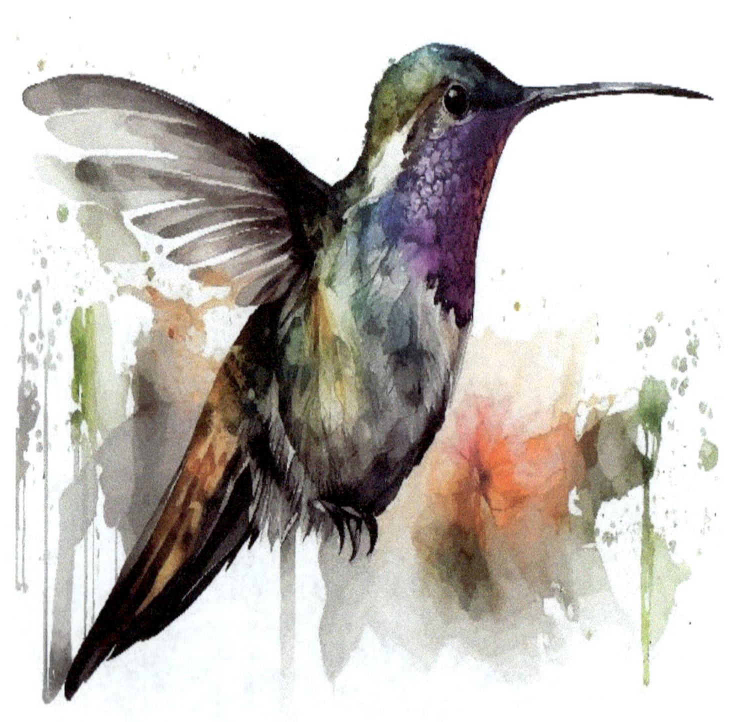

Hope is the thing with feathers that perches in the soul, and sings the tune without words, and never stops at all.

Emily Dickinson

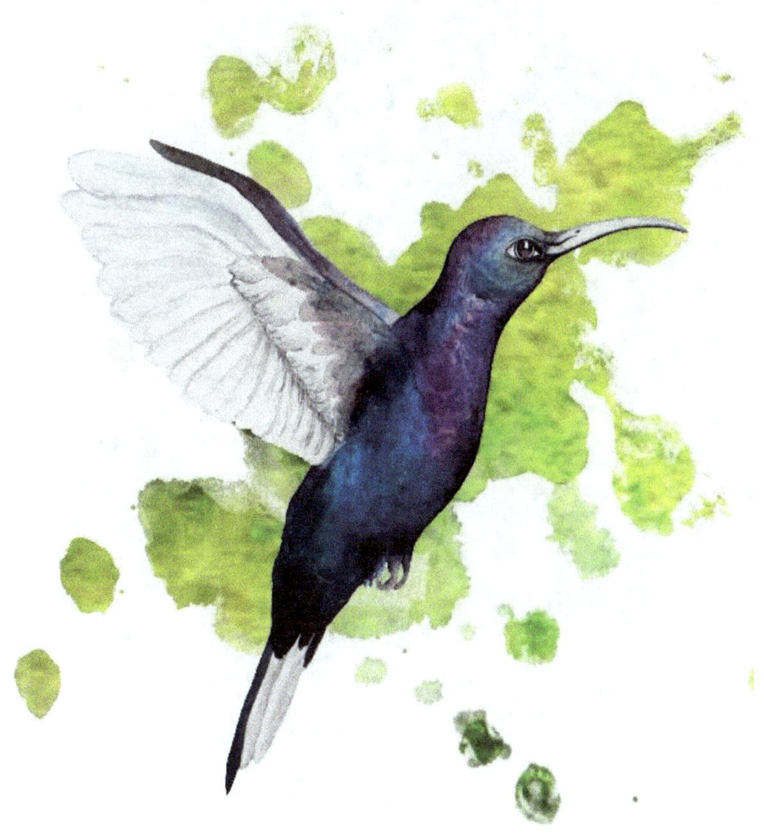

Hope is a good thing, maybe the best of things, and no good thing ever dies.

Stephen King

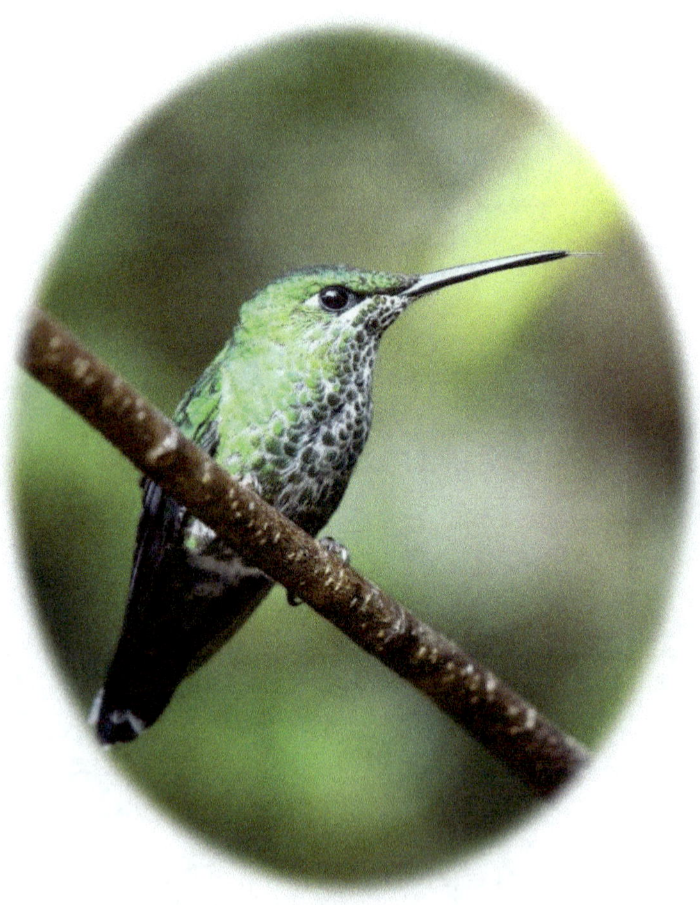

Hope is the anchor of the soul, the stimulus to action, and the incentive to achievement.

Unknown

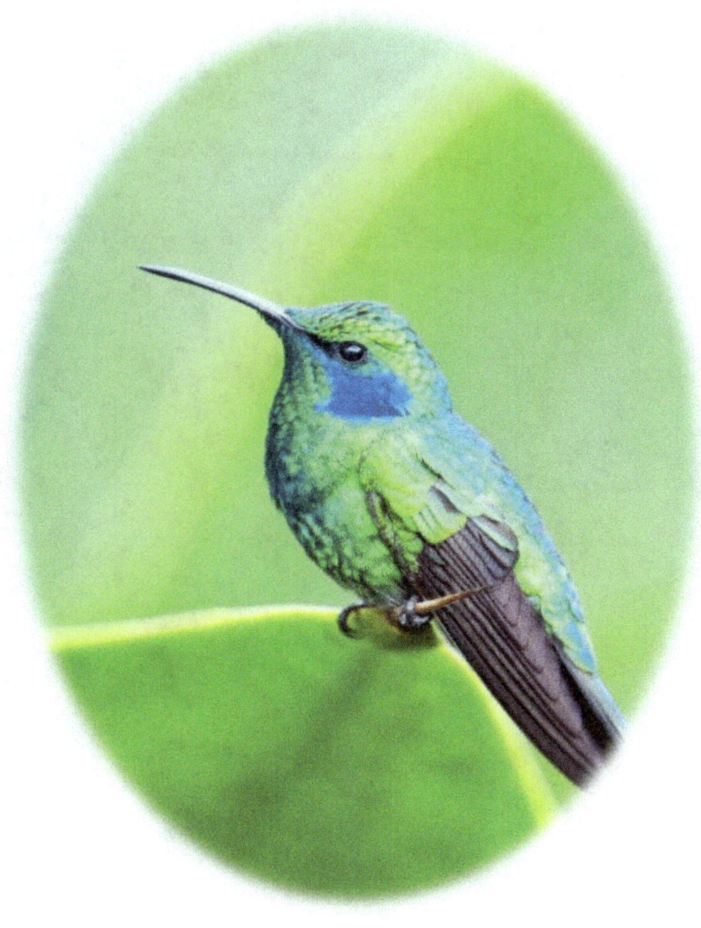

Hope is the only thing stronger than fear.

Suzanne Collins

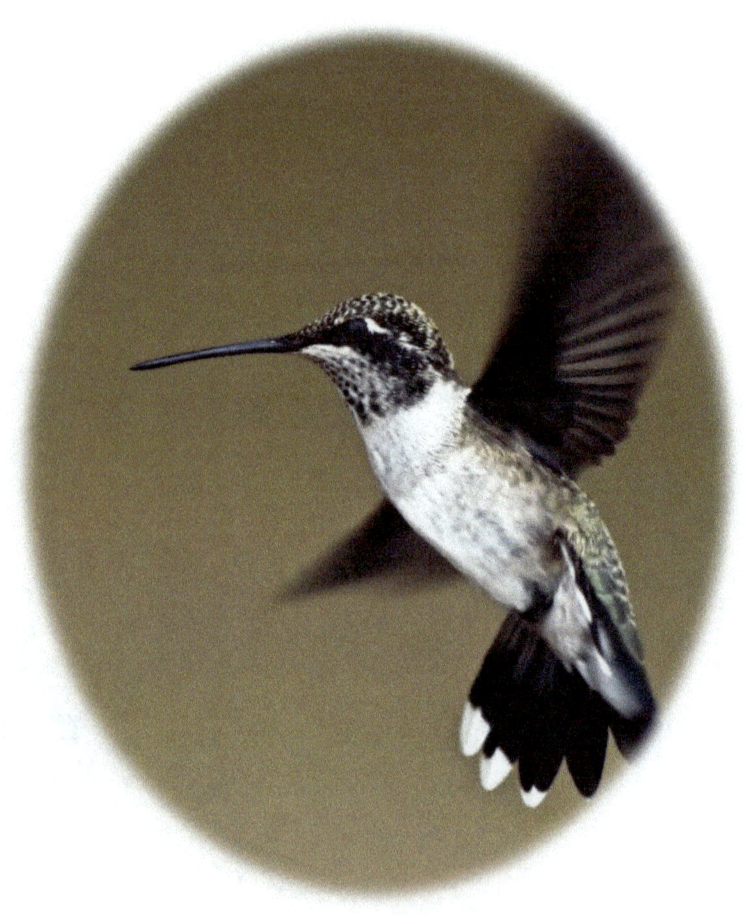

Hope is a force of nature. Don't let anyone tell you different.

Jim Butcher

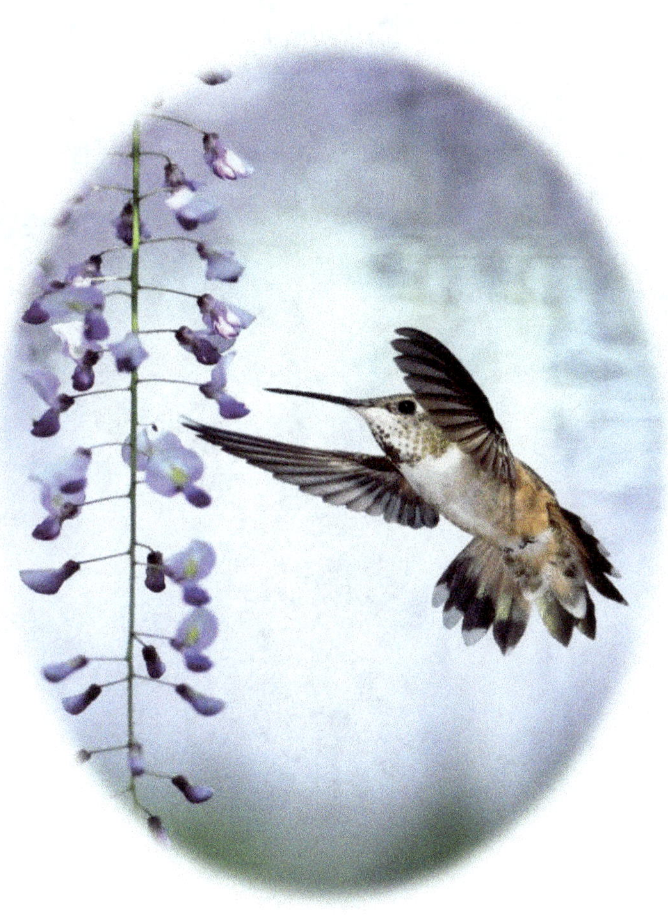

Hope is not about transforming reality overnight; it is about inspiring people to believe that a better tomorrow is possible.

Unknown

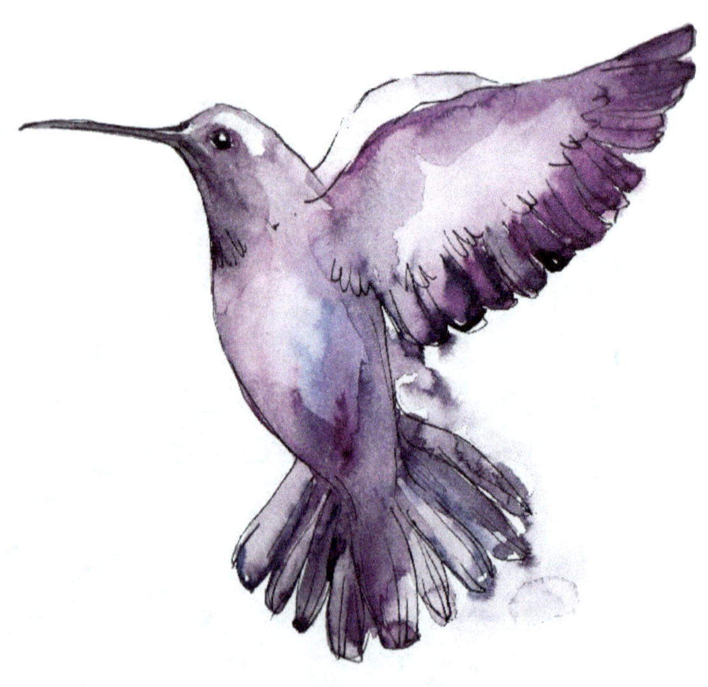

Hope doesn't easily give out, or in, or up. It holds on. It keeps keeping on. It keeps us going even when logic tells us to give up. Hope presses us forward, even when things seem stark or impossible.

Connie Kerbs

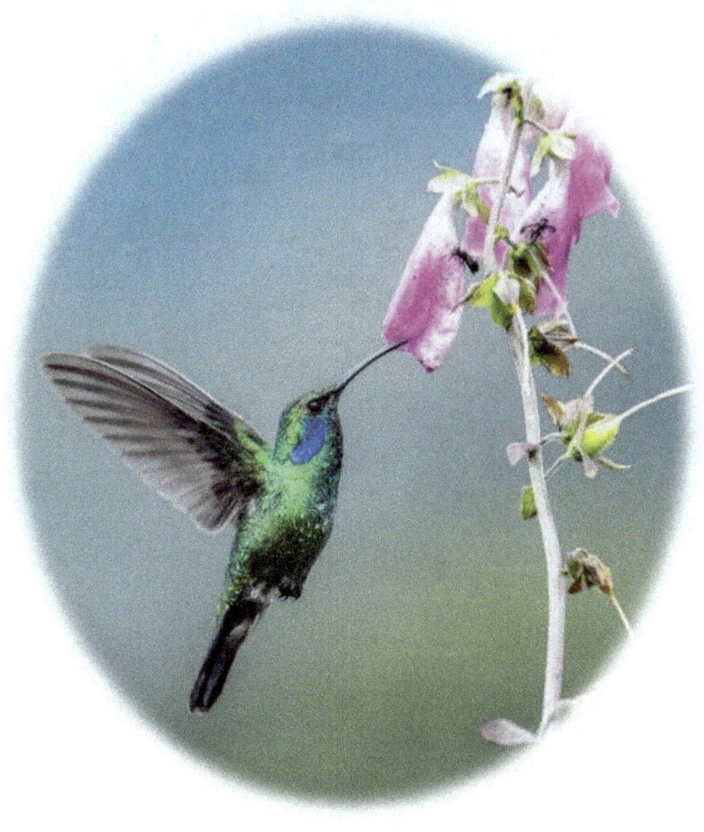

Hope doesn't come from calculating whether the good news is winning out over the bad. It's simply a choice to take action.

Anna Lappe

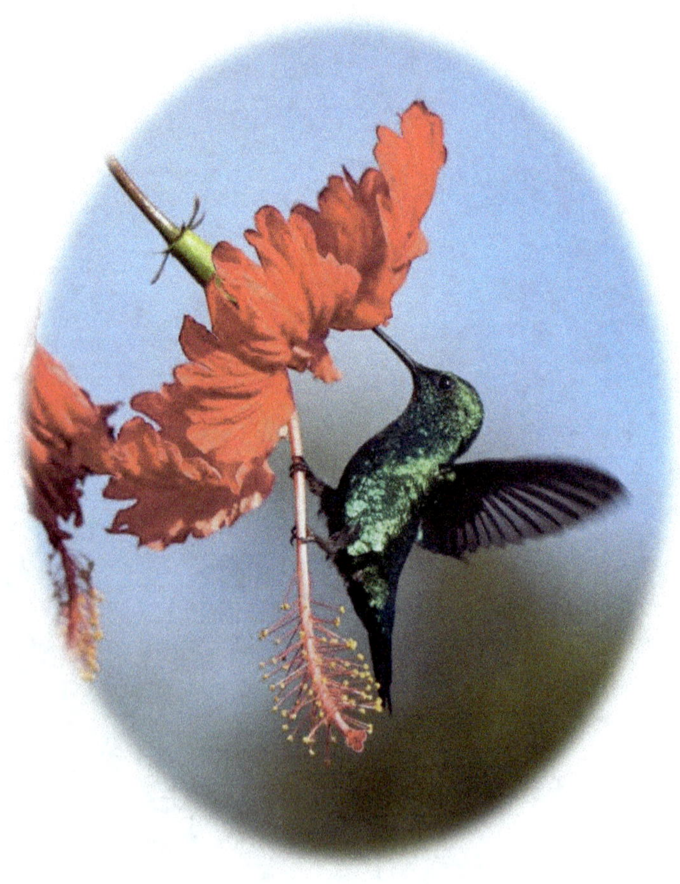

We must accept finite disappointment but
must never lose infinite hope.
Martin Luther King Jr.

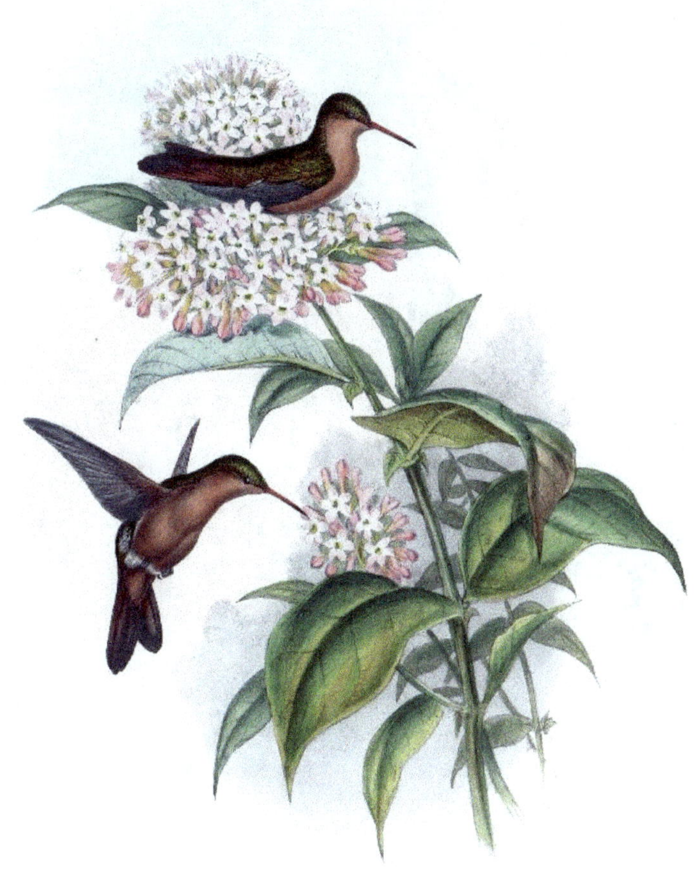

Hope begins in the dark, the stubborn hope that if you just show up and try to do the right thing, the dawn will come.

Anne Lamott

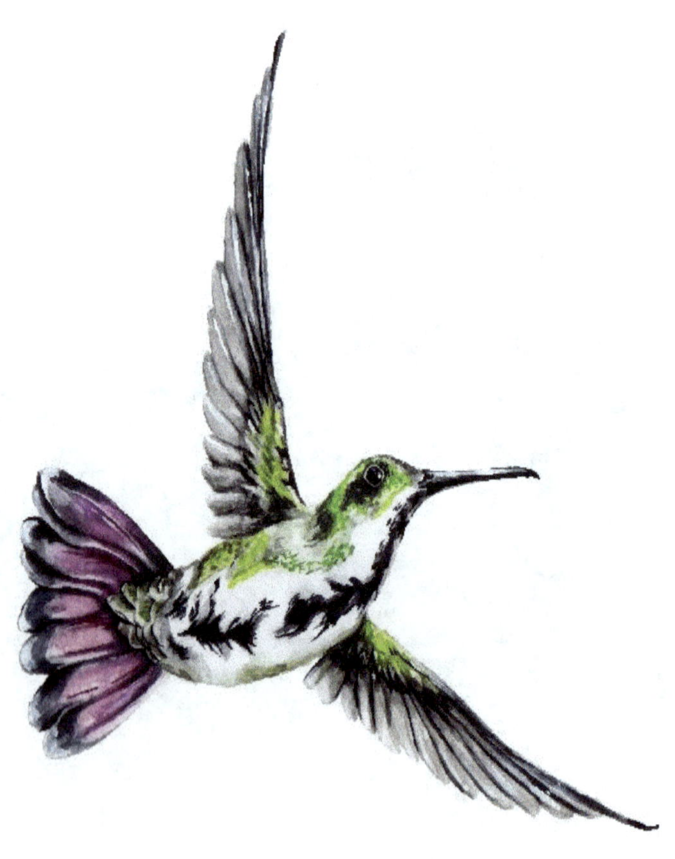

The very least you can do in your life is to figure out what you hope for. And the most you can do is live inside that hope.

Barbara Kingsolver

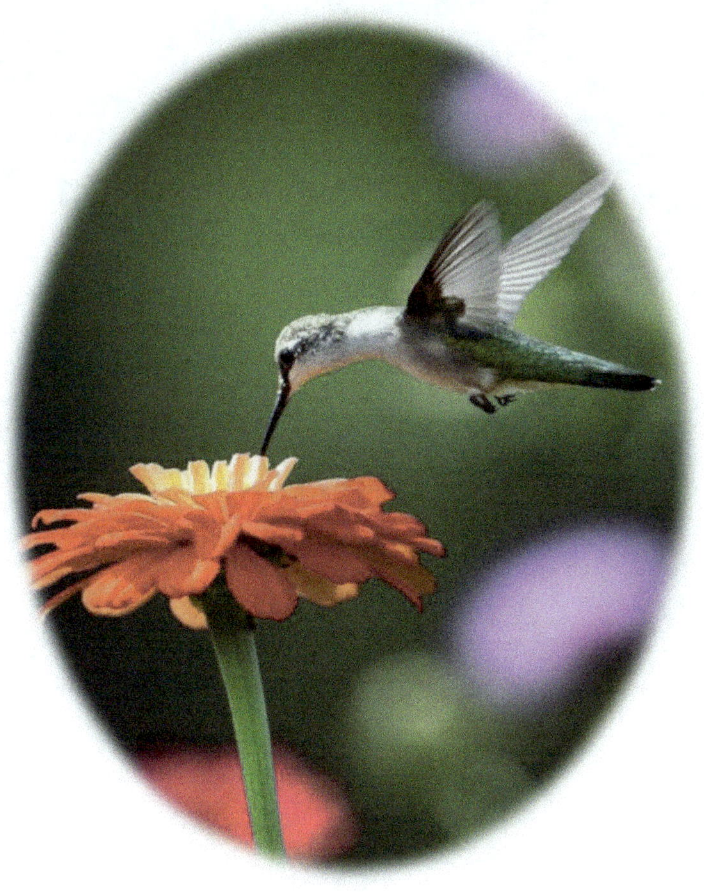

Most of the important things in the world have been accomplished by people who have kept on trying when there seemed to be no hope at all.

Dale Carnegie

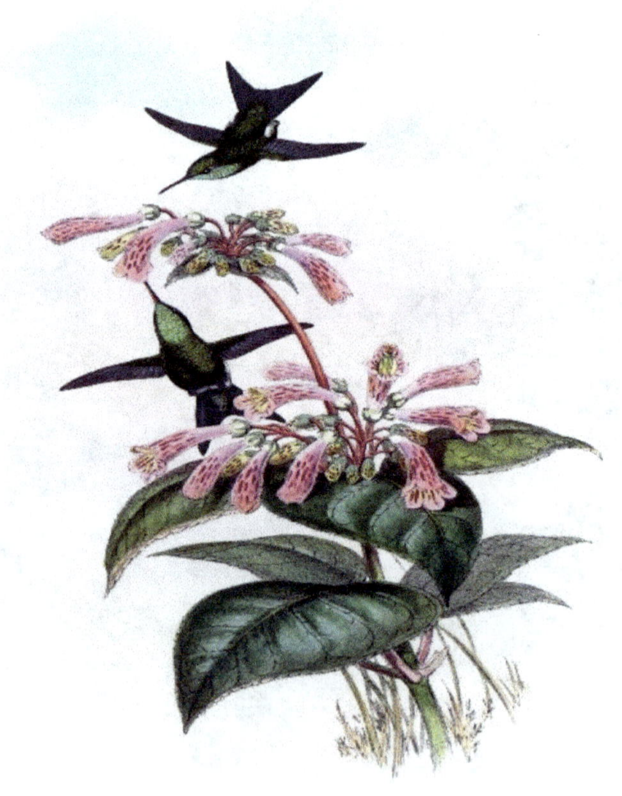

It is because of hope that you suffer. It is through hope that you'll change things.

Maxime Lagacé

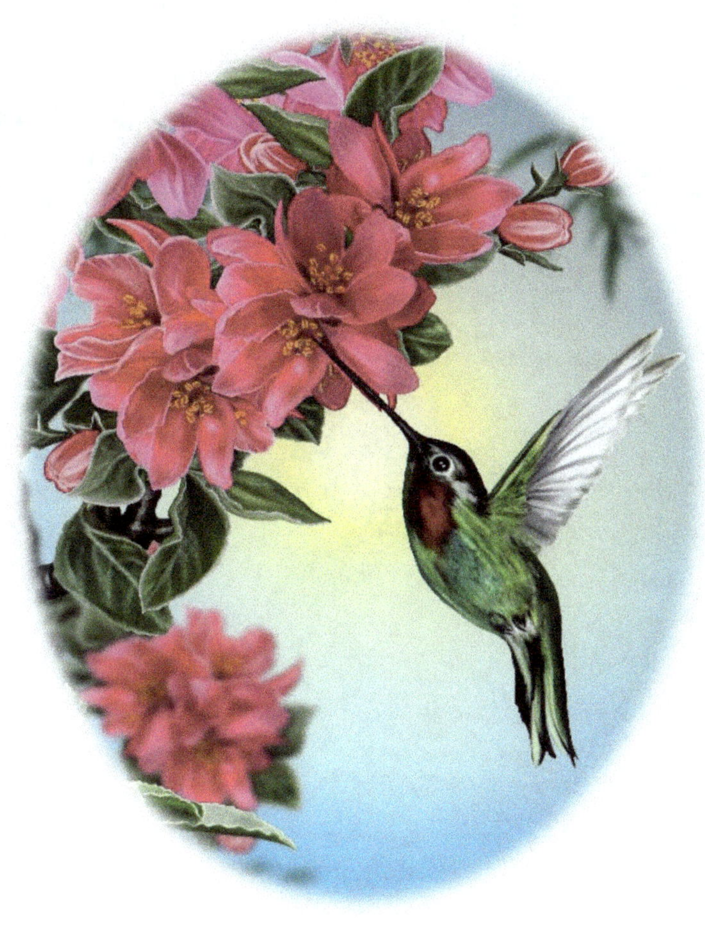

Hope is the spark that ignites change. It's the fire that consumes us with dreams and creative, inspirational notions, and the wherewithal to do something *different* – to make an important, even if difficult - change.

Connie Kerbs

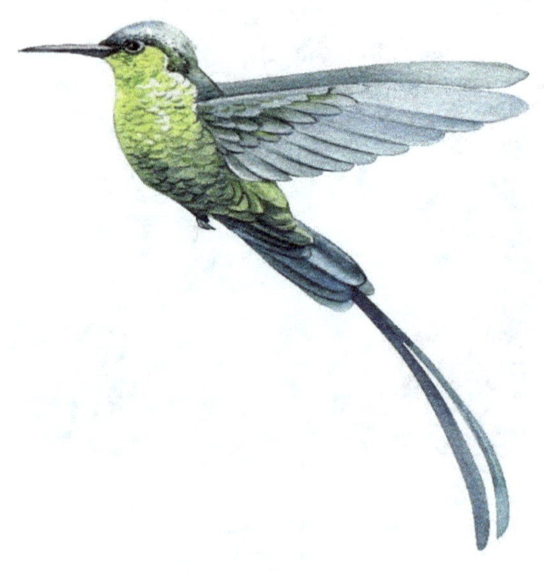

Hope is the fuel that keeps us going, the belief that tomorrow will bring new possibilities and brighter horizons.

Helen Keller

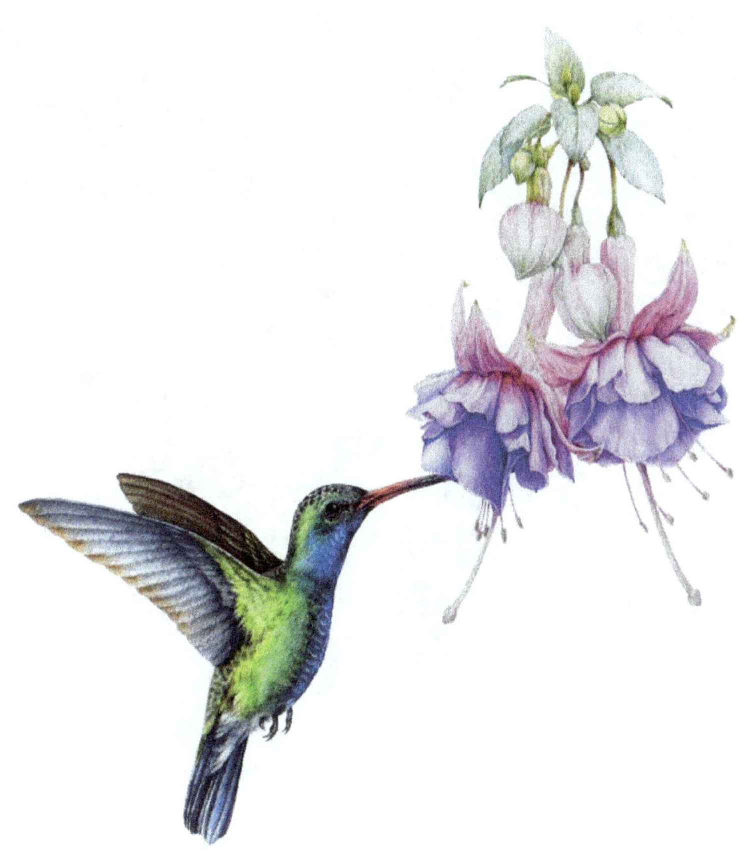

Hope is the heartbeat of the soul, reminding us that even in the darkest of times, there is a flicker of light waiting to ignite.

Unknown

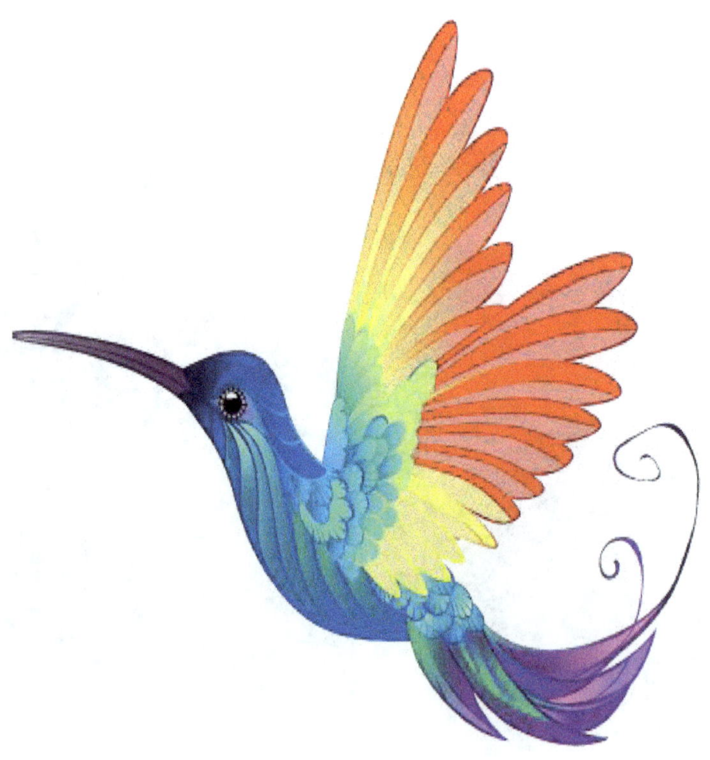

Every great dream begins with a dreamer.
Always remember, you have within you
the strength, the patience, and the passion
to reach for the stars to change the world.
Harriet Tubman

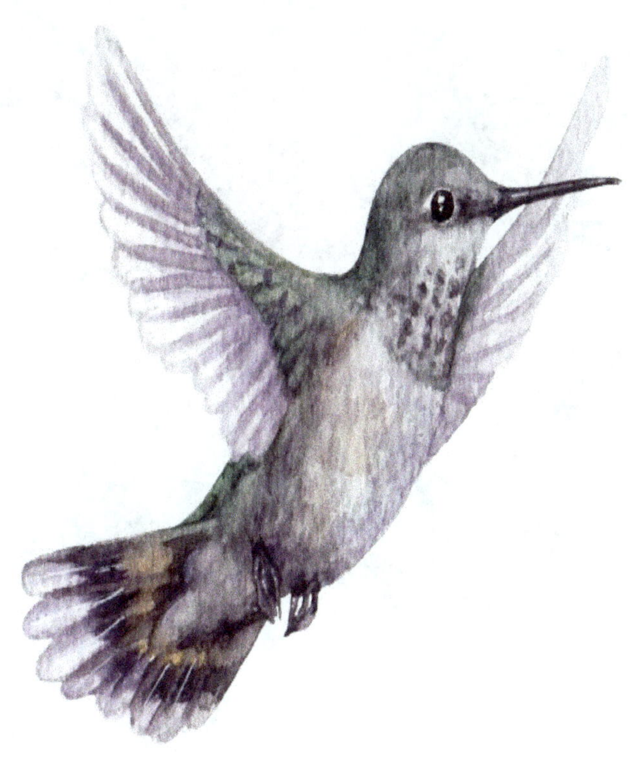

Hope is the secret ingredient that infuses courage into the hearts of those facing adversity, propelling them to rise above their challenges.

Malala Yousafzai

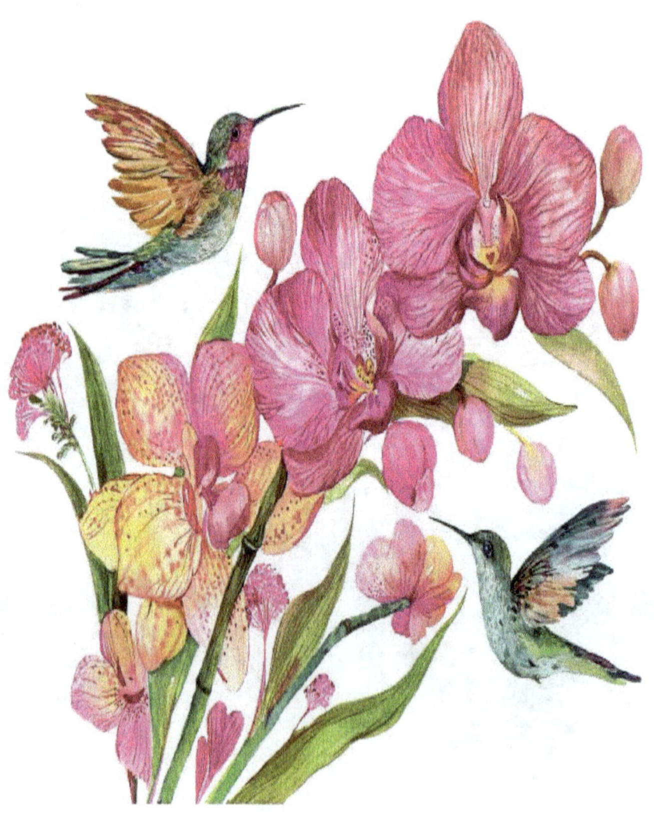

Hope is the vision of what could be, the unwavering faith that our dreams are within reach if we persist and believe.

Nelson Mandela

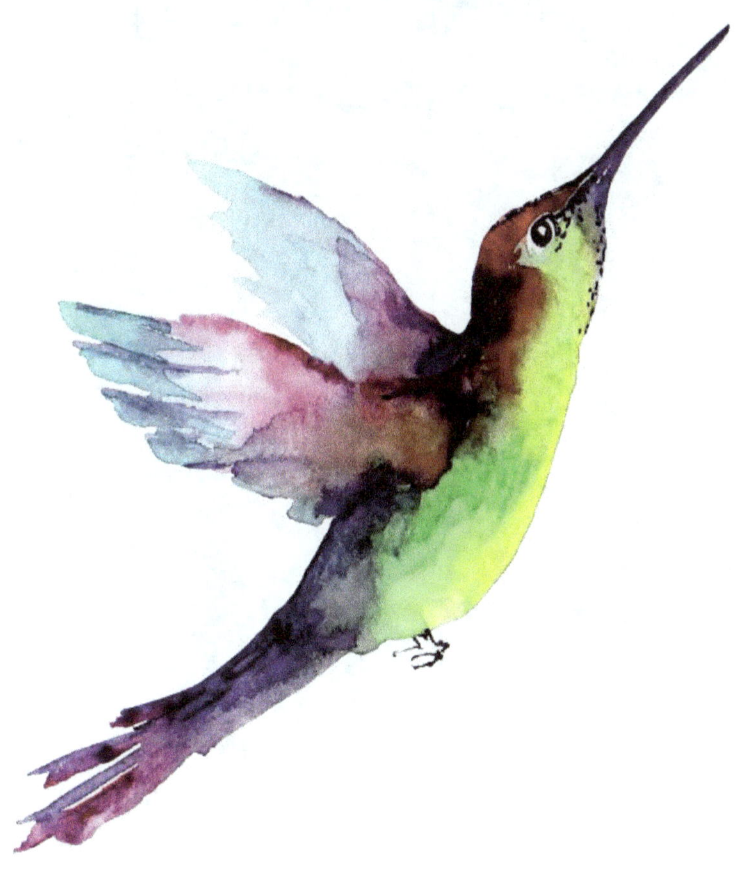

In the middle of difficulty lies opportunity.

Albert Einstein

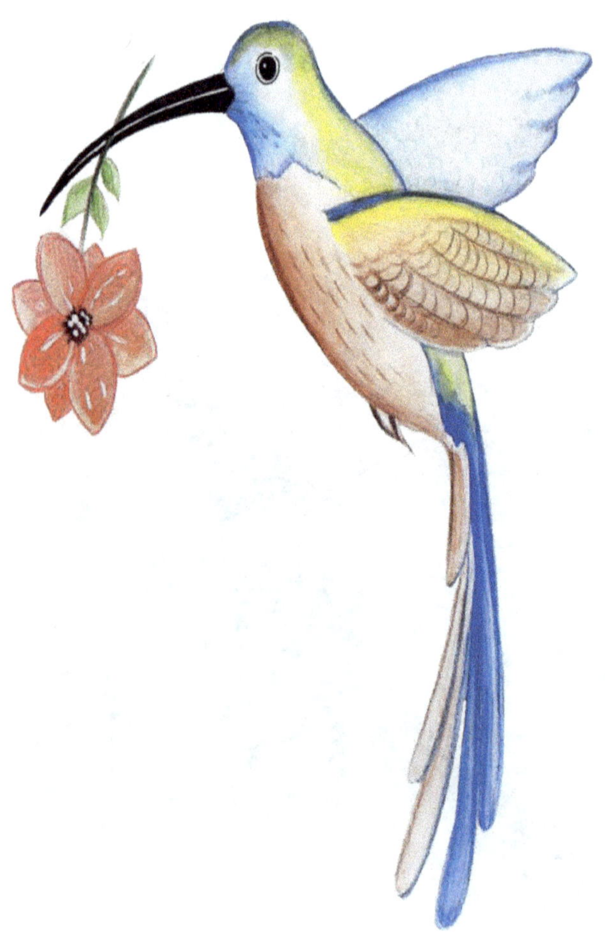

Hope is the song of the heart, resonating
through the trials and tribulations,
reminding us that there is always a melody
of possibility.

Maya Angelou

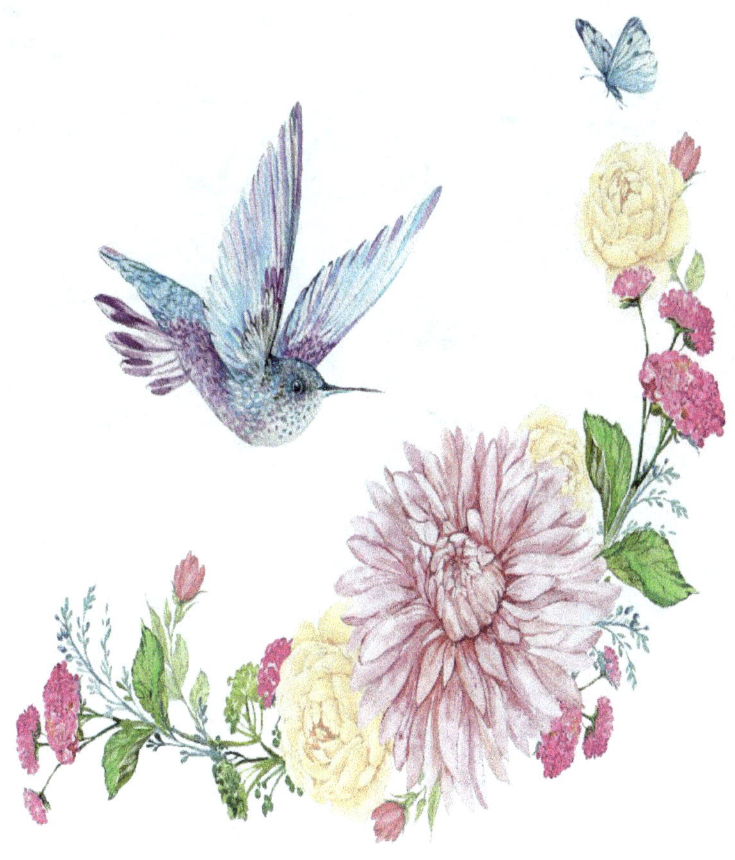

Hope is the compass that guides us through the storms of life, pointing us towards the shores of resilience and renewal.

Martin Luther King Jr.

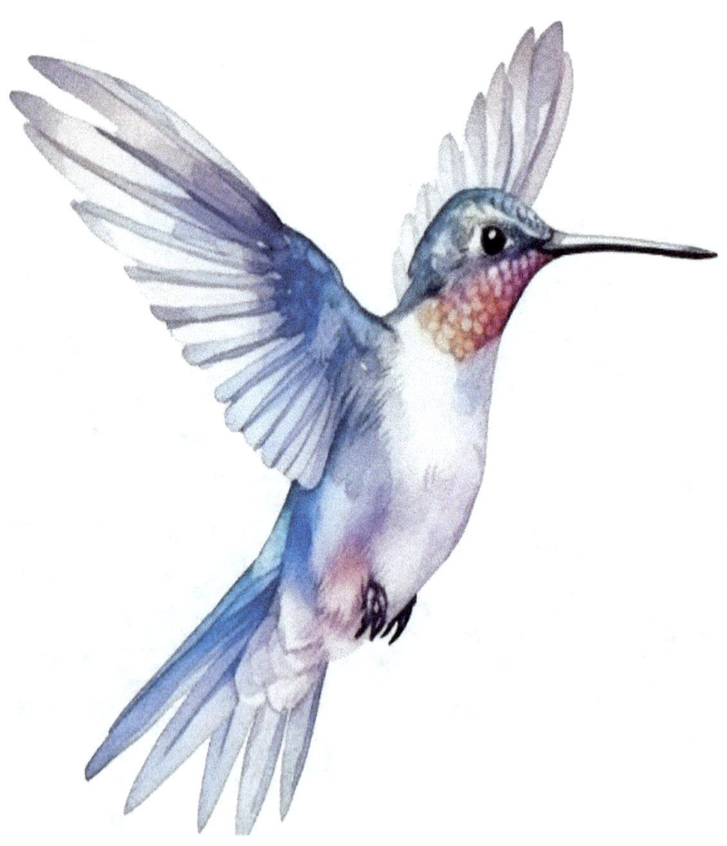

The future belongs to those who believe in the beauty of their dreams.

Eleanor Roosevelt

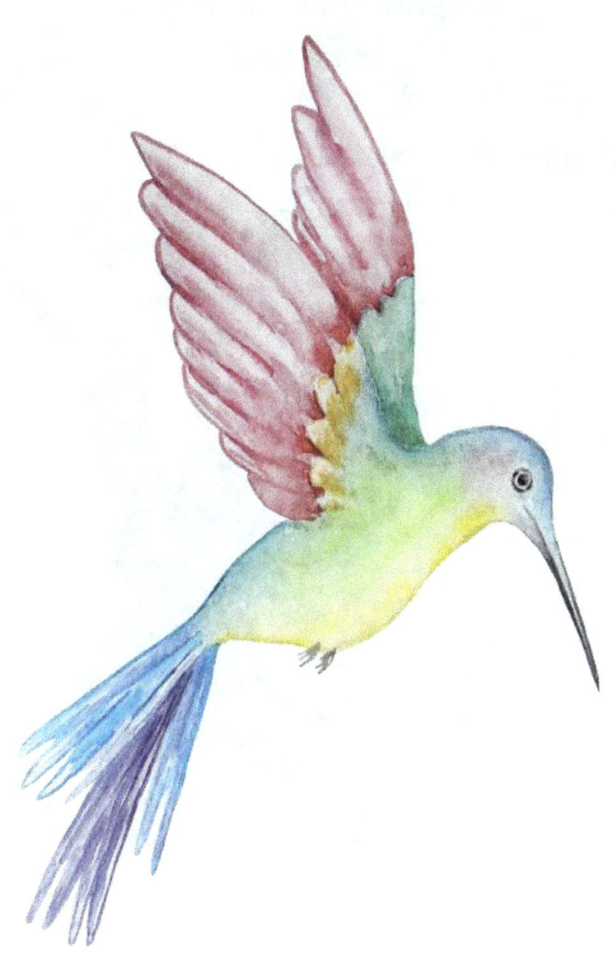

Hope is the path between our yesterdays, todays, and tomorrows. It quilts our patchwork of struggles and joys into a beautiful, connected continuum we can, in the end, make sense of.

Connie Kerbs

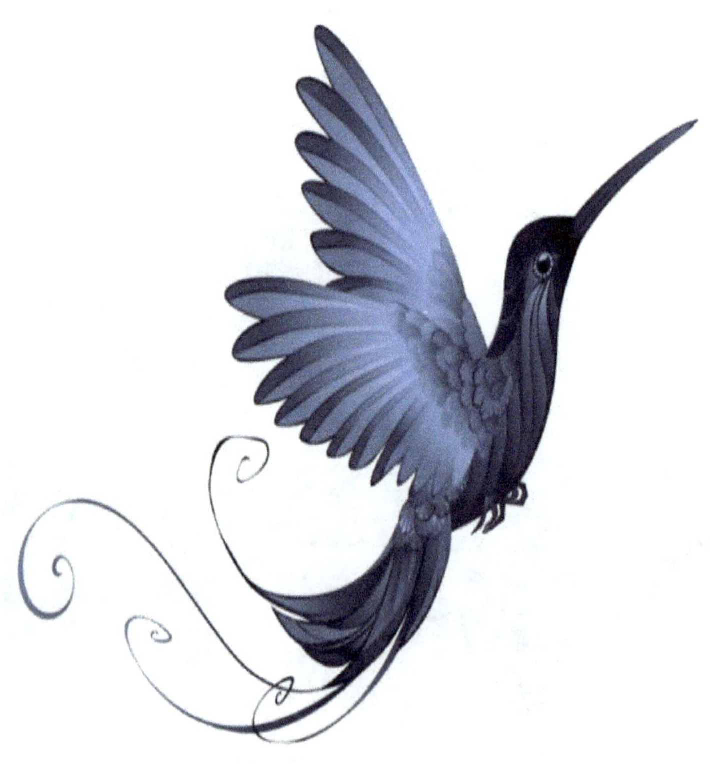

Hope is the whisper that keeps encouraging us when we are discouraged, the internal voice that motivates us when we are deflated, and the fuel that ignites our own internal, eternal flame.

Connie Kerbs

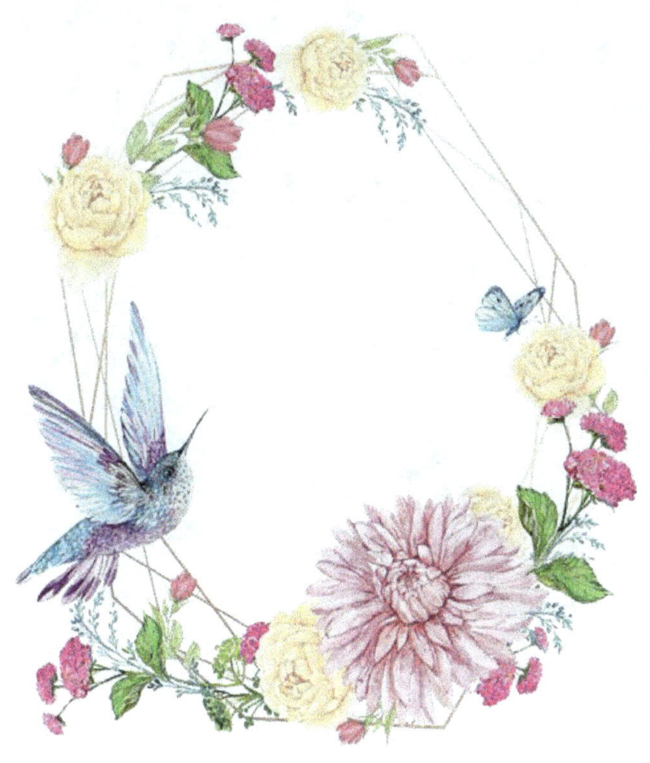

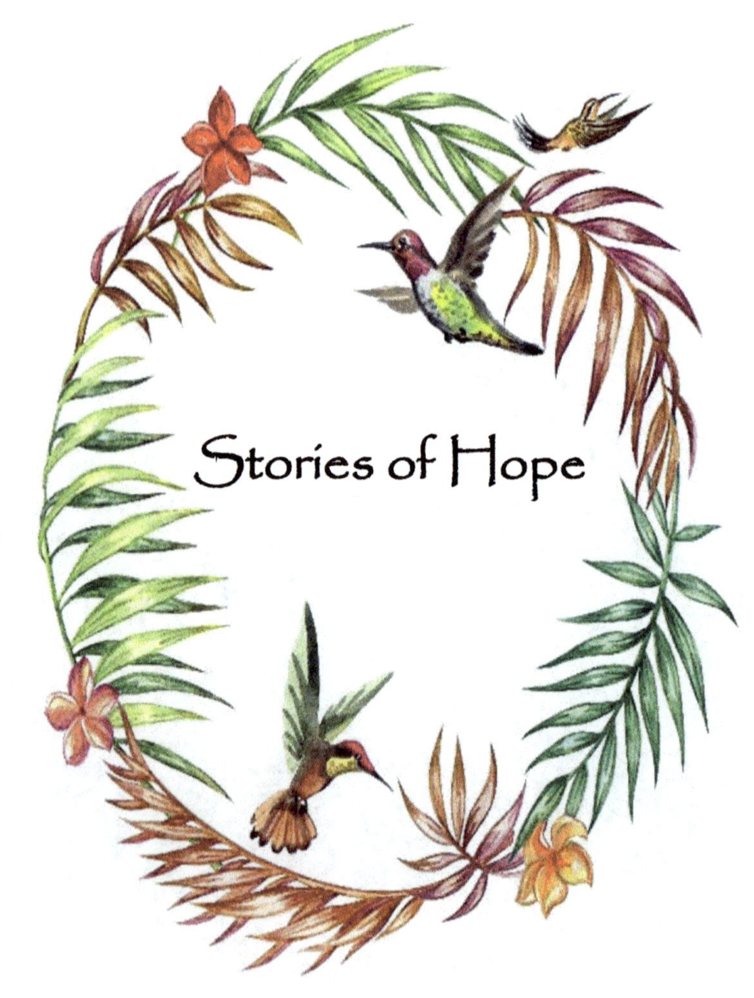

Stories of Hope

The Story of Job

Job was a faithful servant of God who was tested greatly by Satan. He lost his family, wealth, and health, but remained steadfast in his faith and hope in God. Despite his many trials and hardships, Job never lost his hope in God's goodness and love.

Eventually, God restored to Job all that he had lost and blessed him with even more. The story of Job is a powerful reminder that even in the darkest of times, we can never lose our hope in God's faithfulness and love.

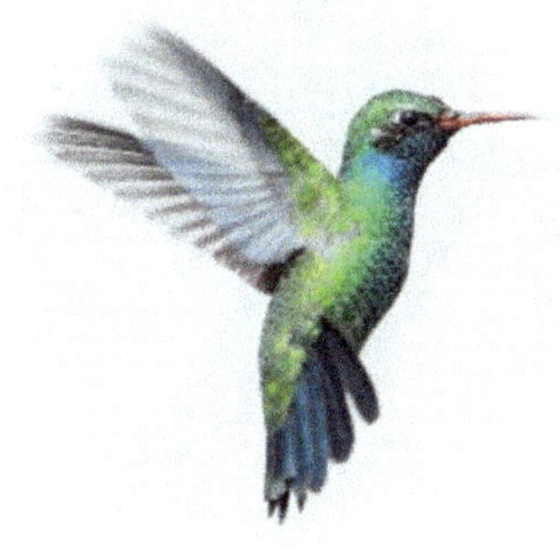

The Story of Joseph

Joseph faced many challenges and setbacks, including being sold into slavery by his own brothers, falsely accused of a crime, and imprisoned for years. Despite these hardships, he remained faithful to God and used his talents to interpret dreams, eventually rising to a position of great importance in Pharaoh's court. Joseph's story demonstrates the power of perseverance, faith, grace - and a spirit of *wise* forgiveness in the face of maltreatment and adversity.

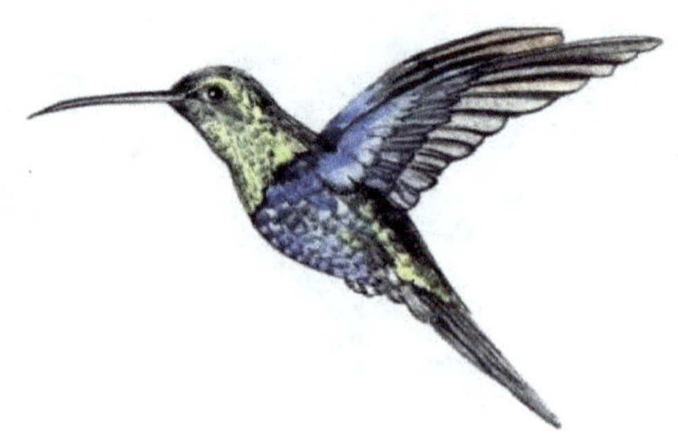

Horatio Spafford:
A Story of Hope

If there is one man who sums up the emotion of hope, it is Horatio Spafford.

Horatio was born in New York in 1828, but it was in Chicago that he and his wife, Anna, made a name for themselves within the Christian community. They were active and valued members of their church, and always opened their door to visitors – no matter who they were, where they came from, or what they looked like.

During their loving marriage, Horatio and Anna welcomed five beautiful children into the world. Unfortunately, Horatio and Anna were struck by a series of tragedies.

At just four years of age, Horatio Jr passed away from scarlet fever. While the family was mourning, just one year later, a big fire swept across Chicago. 300 people lost their lives and Horatio's family saw a number of their properties burned down. But despite losing so much of his wealth, Horatio still dedicated his time to helping those in need.

Two years later, Horatio and Anna planned to take their four daughters on a trip to England. Anna took the children across on a ship while Horatio was delayed with work, but the boat was involved in a crash and all four daughters perished. Somehow, Anna managed to survive by floating on a plank of wood all the way to Cardiff in Wales.

It was on his way to meet his wife, while passing by the exact spot where his daughters passed away that Horatio wrote his world-famous hymn, *It Is Well With My Soul*.

Even though Horatio and Anna had gone through such tragedy, their hearts and souls were still filled with *hope*. Because they knew that God had a plan for their five children in heaven. And they also knew that Anna had been saved for a reason – to do good on Earth.

Horatio and Anna eventually moved to Jerusalem where they took in homeless children, cared for the sick, and helped the needy. They had three more children, although their next son also passed away at the age of four. However, no matter what obstacles they faced, Horatio and Anna always used hope as their fuel to keep going and to keep making a positive difference in people's lives.

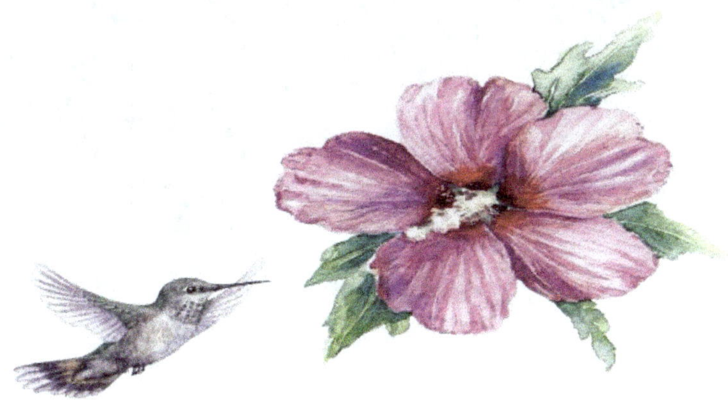

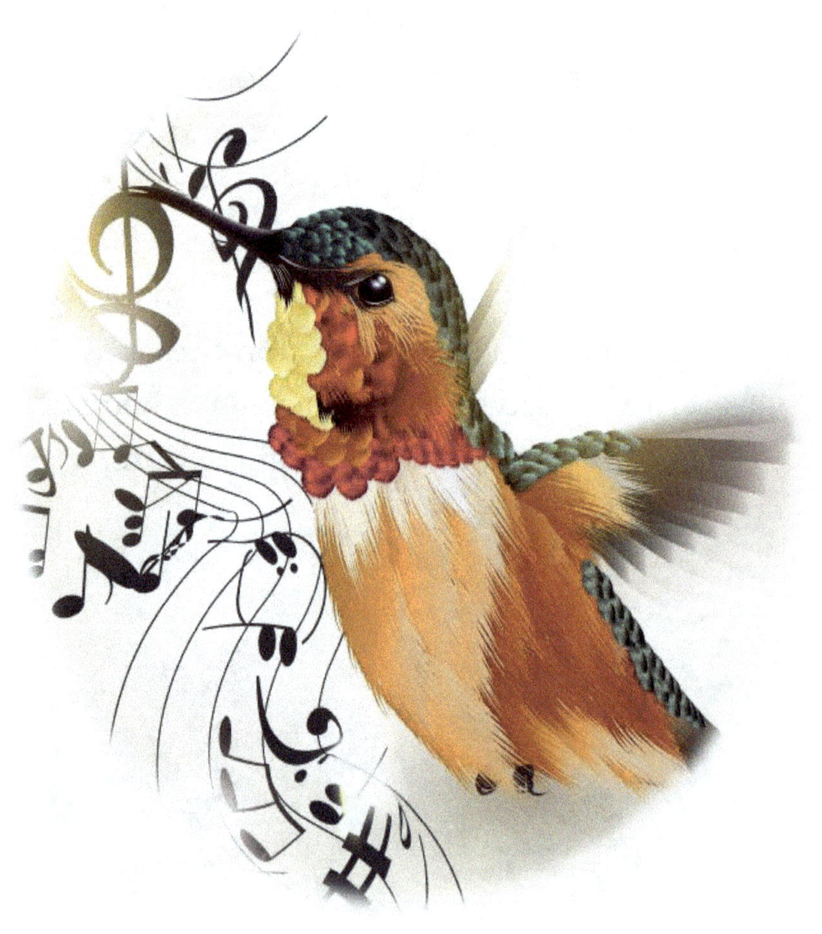

It is Well with My Soul (1876)

When peace like a river, attendeth my way,
When sorrows like sea billows roll;
Whatever my lot, Thou hast taught me to know[b]
It is well, it is well, with my soul.

Refrain
It is well, (it is well),
With my soul, (with my soul)
It is well, it is well, with my soul.

Though Satan should buffet,
though trials should come,
Let this blest assurance control,
That Christ has regarded my helpless estate,
And hath shed His own blood for my soul.

My sin, oh, the bliss of this glorious thought!
My sin, not in part but the whole,
Is nailed to the cross, and I bear it no more,
Praise the Lord, praise the Lord, O my soul!

For me, be it Christ, be it Christ hence to live:
If Jordan above me shall roll,
No pang shall be mine, for in death as in life,
Thou wilt whisper Thy peace to my soul.

But Lord, 'tis for Thee, for Thy coming we wait,
The sky, not the grave, is our goal;
Oh, trump of the angel! Oh, voice of the Lord!
Blessed hope, blessed rest of my soul.

And Lord, haste the day
when the faith shall be sight,
The clouds be rolled back as a scroll;
The trump shall resound,
and the Lord shall descend,
A song in the night, oh my soul!

2023 is the 150th anniversary of *It Is Well with My Soul*. Commemoration services are being planned to remember the actual day of the tragedy, Wednesday November 22nd, and a new edition of the book, *It Is Well with My Soul: From Tragedy to Trust* has also been published in the anniversary year.

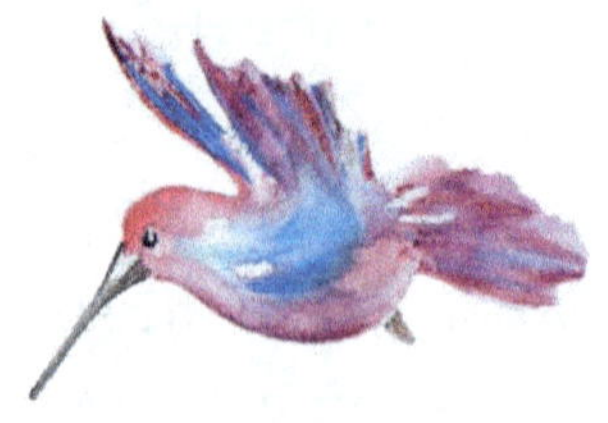

The Unlucky Rabbit: A Tale of Hope

In the village of Meadowbrook lived a young rabbit named Oliver. Oliver felt like an outsider in Meadowbrook because nothing ever went right for him. Oliver faced constant misfortune while the other rabbits enjoyed good fortune and delight. The carrot crops of his fellow rabbits thrived while his own struggled to grow. Their fur was shiny and sleek, while his was perpetually unruly. Anytime Oliver had a picnic, it rained on him.

One morning, as Oliver hopped along the village path, he chanced upon a peculiar coin with an inscription that read, "Hope brings luck to those who believe." Intrigued by its promise, Oliver kept the coin, believing it might bring luck to his troubled days. Carefully, he tucked it into his pocket and continued on his way. Unknown to the unlucky rabbit, a small hole in his pocket allowed the coin to slip away.

From that day forward, Oliver noticed his luck began to grow. Once struggling, his garden now flourished. His bountiful crop won him a prize at the county fair. People began to notice him, offering kind words and invitations to tea. His fur seemed to lay better, and rather than being rained on, the sun shined on his picnics! Oliver was glad he found that lucky coin.

One day, while in the forest near the village, Oliver discovered another coin on the path near the very spot where he had found the first one. Excited that he had discovered another lucky coin, Oliver eagerly picked it up and reached into his pocket to compare the two. However, much to his surprise, the only thing he found in his pocket was a hole.

At that moment, Oliver had a sudden realization. It was not the coin that brought him luck but rather the hope it had inspired. His hope for a brighter future had transformed his life. The coin had done nothing but spark the power within him.

He decided to leave the coin on the forest path, symbolizing hope for someone else. With his newfound wisdom, Oliver understood he didn't need the physical token. His own hope would guide him, bringing him fortune and joy. And so, he set off, spreading hope wherever he went.

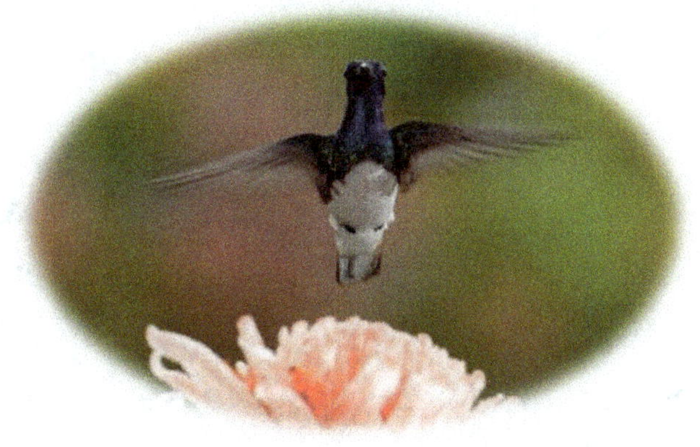

Resilience in the Shadows:
A Journey of Hope

In the lively city of Beirut, a young boy was born into a world of humble beginnings. When he was just three years old, his parents split up, and his father, caught up in drugs, ended up in prison. Meanwhile, his mother went through three troubled marriages, which led to frequent moves that made his teenage years unstable. Changing schools became a common occurrence for the boy, who eventually dropped out of high school at 17.

He didn't let these setbacks stop him. He discovered a passion for hockey and showed incredible talent as a goalkeeper. Unfortunately, a serious injury dashed his hopes of a successful hockey career. Nevertheless, he kept going, determined to overcome these unexpected challenges.

As time passed, the boy grew into a resilient man, and his life changed directions when his sister was diagnosed with the deadly blood cancer, Leukemia. He sold his house to be closer to her, took care of her home, cooked her meals, and helped with her medications. Tragedy struck again when his closest friend passed away, leaving a hole in his heart. The weight of grief burdened him greatly.

In the following years, he found solace in the love of his girlfriend. However, their happiness was devastated one Christmas Eve when they experienced the heartbreak of losing a stillborn daughter. This loss strained their relationship and led to a period of separation. But after taking time to heal, their love brought them back together, stronger than before. Unfortunately, fate dealt another cruel blow when his girlfriend tragically died in a car accident, plunging him into unimaginable sorrow.

As he pushed forward, life pushed back; a wildfire swept through his home, destroying most of his belongings and precious memories.

Despite facing unimaginable heartbreak and loss, the man clung to a glimmer of hope, refusing to give up on the belief that better days were possible. With unwavering determination, he forged an extraordinary path for himself.

Today, Keanu Reeves' success as an actor has allowed him to make a positive impact on the lives of others. He has dedicated himself to philanthropic efforts, using his passion for helping people. His story serves as a symbol of hope, showcasing how one can overcome tragedy and emerge stronger. His legacy is one of resilience, kindness, and unwavering hope, proving that hope has the power to transform lives.

So, the next time you find yourself in the depths of despair, remember Keanu Reeves' journey and let his story remind you that hope is a beacon that shines brightest in the face of adversity.

"Much of my appreciation of life has come through loss. Life is precious. It's worthwhile." - Keanu Reeves

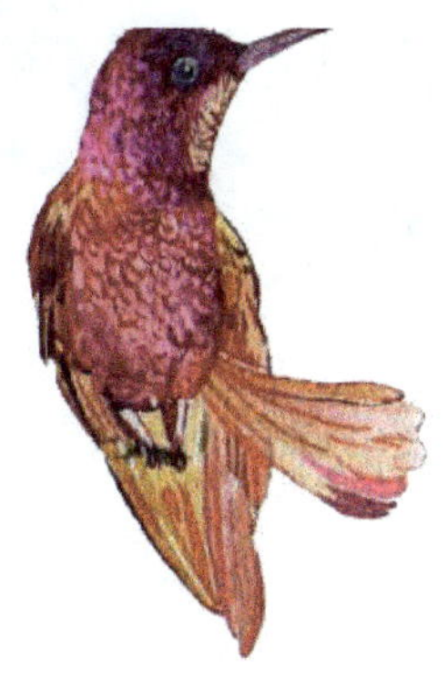

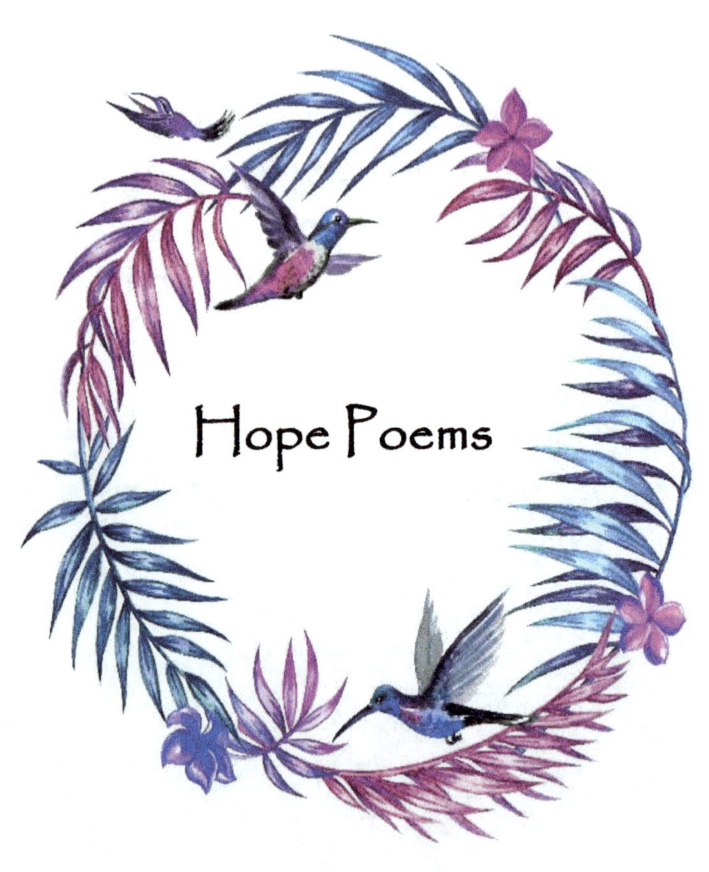

Hope Poems

The Wind of Sorrow

The Wind of Sorrow touched my life today;
I felt his cold grey wings beside me pass,
And shuddered at the chill November day,
While leaves fell withering in the withering
grass.
Then I saw, through tears that dimmed my sight,
How, in the naked beauty of each tree,
The Wind of Sorrow, walking in his might,
Had stripped the branches of their vanity.
He took away the gold and purple dress,
And left the slender limbs without a stain,
Whiter than birch-bark in their nakedness,
And beauteous still, in outline and in grain
.So in my heart there grew a newer hope,
And strength to bear the burden of the day;
For Sorrow's wind had blown away the scope
Of things that charmed my sight and led astray.
And now, within my soul's November time,
I strip the tinsel off my aims and plans,
And let the Wind of Sorrow, in his prime,
Do with me what the Master Will commands.

Henry Van Dyke

A Psalm of Life

Tell me not, in mournful numbers,
Life is but an empty dream!
For the soul is dead that slumbers,
And things are not what they seem.

Life is real! Life is earnest!
And the grave is not its goal;
Dust thou art, to dust returnest,
Was not spoken of the soul.

Not enjoyment, and not sorrow,
Is our destined end or way;
But to act, that each to-morrow
Find us farther than to-day.

Art is long, and Time is fleeting,
And our hearts, though stout and brave,
Still, like muffled drums, are beating
Funeral marches to the grave.

In the world's broad field of battle,
In the bivouac of Life,
Be not like dumb, driven cattle!
Be a hero in the strife!

Trust no Future, howe'er pleasant!
Let the dead Past bury its dead!
Act,— act in the living Present!
Heart within, and God o'erhead!

Lives of great men all remind us
We can make our lives sublime,
And, departing, leave behind us
Footprints on the sands of time;—

Footprints, that perhaps another,
Sailing o'er life's solemn main,
A forlorn and shipwrecked brother,
Seeing, shall take heart again.

Let us, then, be up and doing,
With a heart for any fate;
Still achieving, still pursuing,
Learn to labor and to wait.

Henry Wadsworth Longfellow

If

If you can keep your head when all about you
Are losing theirs and blaming it on you,
If you can trust yourself when all men doubt you,
But make allowance for their doubting too;
If you can wait and not be tired by waiting,
Or being lied about, don't deal in lies,
Or being hated, don't give way to hating,
And yet don't look too good, nor talk too wise:

If you can dream—and not make dreams your
master;
If you can think—and not make thoughts your
aim;

If you can meet with Triumph and Disaster
And treat those two impostors just the same;
If you can bear to hear the truth you've spoken
Twisted by knaves to make a trap for fools,
Or watch the things you gave your life to, broken,
And stoop and build 'em up with worn-out tools:

If you can make one heap of all your winnings
And risk it on one turn of pitch-and-toss,
And lose, and start again at your beginnings
And never breathe a word about your loss;

If you can force your heart and nerve and sinew
To serve your turn long after they are gone,
And so hold on when there is nothing in you
Except the Will which says to them: 'Hold on!'

If you can talk with crowds and keep your virtue,
Or walk with Kings—nor lose the common touch,
If neither foes nor loving friends can hurt you,
If all men count with you, but none too much;
"If you can talk with crowds and keep your virtue,

Or walk with Kings—nor lose the common touch,
If neither foes nor loving friends can hurt you,
If all men count with you, but none too much;
If you can fill the unforgiving minute
With sixty seconds' worth of distance run –
Yours is the Earth and everything that's in it,
And – which is more – you'll be a Man my son!"

Rudyard Kipling

“Hope" Is The Thing With Feathers

"Hope" is the thing with feathers -
That perches in the soul -
And sings the tune without the words -
And never stops - at all -

And sweetest - in the Gale - is heard -
And sore must be the storm -
That could abash the little Bird
That kept so many warm -

I've heard it in the chillest land -
And on the strangest Sea -
Yet - never - in Extremity,
It asked a crumb - of me.

Emily Dickinson

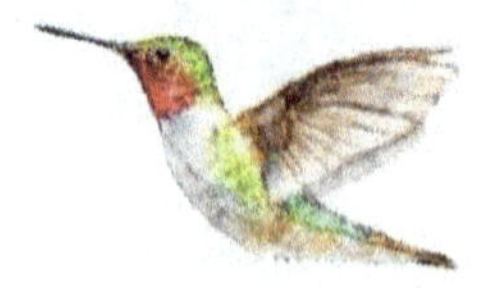

The Amazing Avah Grace

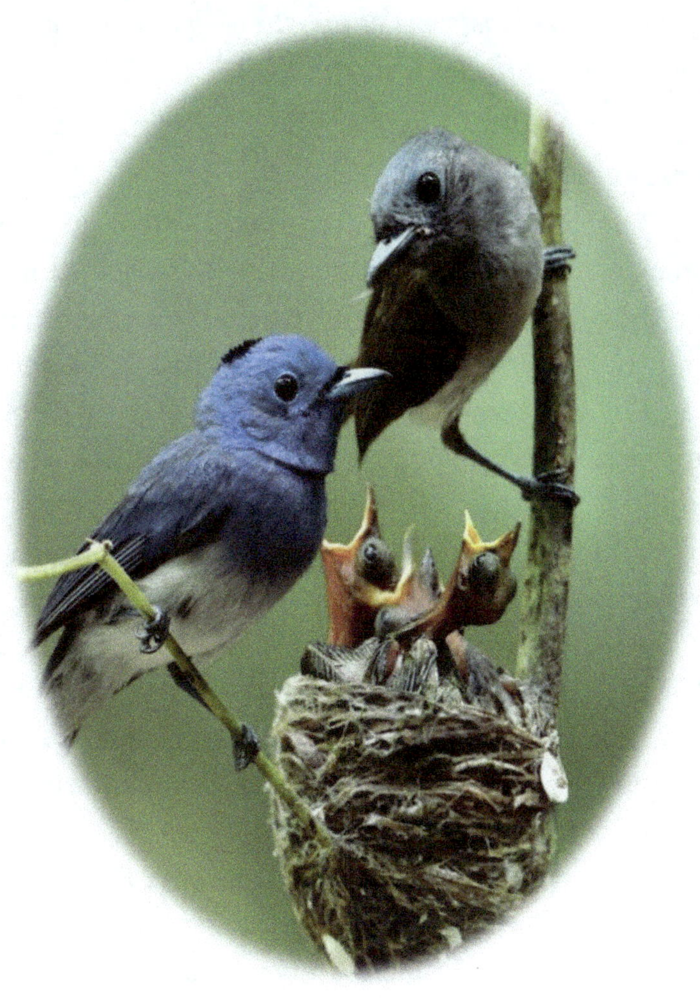

The courageous baby Avah endured unimaginable suffering. After barely surviving against all odds, a little humming literally saved her, and that was just the beginning. This is some of her story, and a few of the many tender miracles surrounding it.

Preface

My husband and I's shared joy in music was a precious facet of our childhood, and in fact is how we met – first in an all-city elementary orchestra, and then later it would reunite us in high school concert and jazz band. This set the stage for the importance of quality music education in what would become our uniquely *large,* (foster-adopt/bio), family. At the time of this story, the beginning of Avah's entrance into our life (as well as the beginning of her life) – we had been married 27 years. We had *long* been foster/adopt parents, and now legally answered to a whopping 15 other people who called us their forever mom and dad – several by now who were all grown up..

By September, 2011, (when Avah was 2 months old) we had fostered dozens of children over a 20+ year span of being a specialized, therapeutic foster home. Children of all ages, stages, and trials had graced our home. With three biological children by then, born smack in the middle of our foster/adopt life, and twelve others ultimately adopted, by then our *fifteen* children included <u>eight</u> full-grown adults, and <u>seven</u> younger ones still at home. Phew. (It's a lot to explain – not alone LIVE!)

All along we have felt that the therapeutic, enriching benefits of music keenly contributed (along with a few other key elements, such as our walk of faith) to our success with many special needs and extraordinary children. Music had also been a source of great joy, as our home ever rang with nursery music, classics, hymns, instruments of all kinds, and singing. Suzuki ear training was a mainstay. Even by then, we felt we had already been privy to many *music-miracles* through the years.

And then came Avah.

Dark Beginnings

Avah's story unfolds heavily, with a sobering subject: a uniquely tragic kind of abuse – infant abuse known as shaken baby syndrome, which results in head trauma and its catastrophic effects in the young victims who endure it.

Avah's heart wrenching experience touched us deeply. She was born normal, healthy, with shining eyes, and a bright smile. But it was *all* cruelly taken from her. At only a few weeks old, she sustained the severest injuries possible to survive. Several tiny ribs were fractured, and she endured multiple, untreated, severe head injuries over several episodes of violence – which all occurred between 3 and 5 weeks old.

Upon her arrival at the hospital, in a coma, she wasn't expected to survive. Fast forward several weeks later, she not only survived – but was *thriving*. Well, thriving relative to her injuries – to her *new normal*. The vast medical team involved with her, including a world class pediatric neurologist and surgeon at the helm, literally could not believe her stamina and will to live. It was more than impressive, which encouraged them to keep helping her to fight for her life as much as possible…

Though not actively fostering anymore, due to our extensive experience with extraordinary and high needs children, and lack of availability of anyone else at that particular moment of need, we received a desperate call to do s*hort-term* care for a fragile infant.

Honestly, in the beginning, I was more than reluctant, and initially determined to make a short visit to the hospital, mainly to support and facilitate getting others onboard. This hesitant posture soon evolved into many long hours in the NICU (Neo-Natal Intensive Care Unit), to familiarize myself with her specific, complex medical needs - in order to help train others.

In the process, I would soon get to know *her*: no small task with a little one now (mostly) blind, (mostly) non-hearing, and on a temporary feeding-tube inserted through the nasal passage, protruding down the esophagus until it was seated confidently in the duodenum, a small bridge between the stomach and the rest of the small intestine.

Difficult Decisions

I soon learned why the *short-term* reference was used in her initial placement call: this sweet little infant was not expected to live long…

Of course, all of this ushered in a great pause for us, as it would anyone. (Which is why there wasn't a long line-up as there usually was with infants coming into care.) While I could offer Avah my experience, there were at least seven little reasons at home which precluded my bringing a high-needs child into the family fold...especially one who was expected to soon pass away. I mean, at first, it took the breath right out of me thinking of putting that kind of grief, by choice, in the midst of my several young children at home…I resolved to explain this to the case managers involved with her - and leave. (Before I got *too* involved.)

Then, something unexpected happened that gave me a different pause. Or rather, an emotional about face. You see, inconsolable bouts of crying are typical of traumatized, severely distressed babies. There were ways to comfort these children, but it was a process of trial and error, patience, and often just time. While swaddling and rocking are eventually (usually) par for the course I didn't expect my gentle sways to immediately quiet her distraught crying – and they didn't. Then, suddenly, in only a few hours into my peek into her world, while waiting for a potential placement to show up (which didn't) - she suddenly soothed as I softly hummed a favorite hymn while rocking her. And not just for a few minutes – it was a sustained relaxation as she melted into me for hours…

I was surprised, but not as much as the hospital staff who had been caring for her. Prior to her inexplicable quieting to my humming, her chronic crying for weeks could only be settled with powerful drugs. And so, I spent the next several hours cuddling her in the rocking chair. We were constantly interrupted for her to be poked, prodded, adjusted, changed, or for a needed treatment. These necessary disruptions distressed her without fail. It wasn't a fluke, as time and again, she would sooth to my slight rocking and humming – and I couldn't help but notice her preference for one particular song.

Intrigued, I accepted the invitation (more like pleas by the nursing staff) to stay longer, with my supportive husband's help at home. I sat up with her in the rocking chair, humming her back to sleep throughout the night, until my arms were intolerably cramped, by now into the wee hours. Curiously, she preferred the same little tune – which, happened to be a favorite of mine also…

Divine Interventions

After several hours of so easily consoling this previously *inconsolable* infant, I knew my heart was in trouble deep. With the sun's rising, I felt the need to quietly *ponder* all of this. I needed guidance, strength, and wisdom beyond my own capacities.

The hospital's cushioned chapel was a reprieve from the early morning bustle – and rest for my weary shoulders, now fatigued from holding her for nigh to 16 hours nearly straight through…

How could I bring home a fragile baby…one most likely to die? How could I think of putting this trauma on my young children at home?

How would we (I?) manage her intensive care, AND still take good care of all the others depending on me? Making all of this even more difficult, I had learned that as no other capable, willing caregivers seemed to be available, she was slated to soon being put on a hospice track – which would mean comfort measures only…No more life-saving interventions – like feeding tubes, which she currently relied upon… If this strong little one, who had already overcome so much, had any hopes at all of surviving, time was of the essence for her to have an experienced, dedicated advocate: a seasoned foster mom. A surrogate *mother*.

And *I* seemed to be the only one in a position to do this at that pertinent time...

As the gravity of all this burdened heavily upon me while lost in my thoughts in the chapel that day, I will always remember the feeling of its crushing weight being lifted from me. I heard loud and clear, in my head, *"You are needed for this…only you can do this…you have been prepared …you will have all you need…have faith…"* Time to call my husband, my rock, and the loving father of our *fifteen* children… He knew the gist, as I had filled him in over the course of my long visit to the hospital, but what would he say now? To this idea taking root in my heart – that I was supposed to *bring her home*? Surly, he would remind me of our already *very full* house…and *very large* family…

There was a long silence after my brief explanation. Had he hung up? (I couldn't have blamed him!) Finally, after an extra-long pause, he said, *"If we are needed to do this…we have been prepared, and we will have all we need. I know it will all work out with faith."* It was uncanny to me that he spoke aloud the exact thoughts still echoing within me from the chapel. Since I had not shared with him the *specific* details of *that* yet – only the summary of the experience, which had served to solidify my feelings that I was supposed to bring her home to be fostered – how could he have known? Indeed, it felt as if something, in the realm of Divine Intervention was trying to tell us (me?) something.

Long story short, Avah soon came home – to seven young children bursting with delight over her. Even our adult children all immediately considered her *their* baby sister, and they committed wholeheartedly to help us love and protect her, for as long as she needed, no matter how long *or short* that time would be.

Maybe, just maybe, we could do this…

More Miracles

She had to fight hard for her life that first year, and especially those first few weeks and months - facing several surgeries, and serious complications. As her injuries resolved, she was left on a permanent feeding tube, called a G-Tube. Her vision and auditory processing centers were decimated, as well as most upper, connective brain tissue. She had permanent, total vision and hearing loss, and would never walk, talk, run or play…never communicate normally, or laugh or sing…

We counted every day with our little angel a blessing – and loved and cared for her with all we had. Admittedly, we held our breath, ever poised to face the grim outcomes predicted by her medical team… ever caught in that elusive, emotionally exhausting hinge of hoping for the best, but preparing for the worst. After weeks, and eventually months of her ongoing survival, her doctors just shook their heads with – *there is no medical explanation for her still being here...* We were required by her team of experts and social workers to have "end of life planning," and measures in place – formally planned, and filed with all the powers that were… We had to map out and pre-implement the supposed impending funeral arrangements… We had to frequently report on her status, which was often a surprising status quo, or now and again, reflected surprising micro-improvements as measured by any one of the several specialists she regularly saw.

Then, somewhere, in the middle of the many therapies and assessment appointments, complex case management, intermittent crying bouts, her intensive daily care, and exhausting days and nights often rolling into one - we had the privilege of being part of another tender music miracle with Avah.

We were determined to maintain healthy normalcy for our other children as much as possible. For starters, the many music lessons and practice schedules that were routine for our family carried on. Once, when Avah was on my lap, a few feet away from a practicing child, Amazing Grace surprisingly resonated out of my nine-year-old daughter's cello strings, and unexpectedly caught Avah's attention! She turned her head toward the sound which was a first! (The first willful turn of her head!) While unable to *see,* or *hear,* (in the normal sense) within moments, she was smiling! Really smiling! Her FIRST real smile!

For a long while, as long as her favorite song played, Avah seemed to keep *seeking* the sound, and the beautiful smiles kept coming. This was such an important, memorable moment in our lives; a very special miracle to be part of. Avah had smiled. And she had obviously *heard* or *felt* the music! And she ENJOYED it! A complex "neuro thing" none of her care team had thought was even a remote possibility, at least according to her brain scans.

The smiles didn't quit – and over time became genuine laughter. She continued *looking* for sounds, especially music. We discovered she loved *hearing* my husband play the guitar, and she could *hear* the (grand) piano. She would spend many hours on one lap or another at its keyboard. One of our daughters in particular, especially enjoyed regularly practicing the piano with little Avah on her lap. A little Avah that responded and rewarded such things with immense joy.

About our grand piano: It had been a dream planted in our youth orchestra and band-primed hearts, and then fertilized when we happened upon a piano convention put on by a local music college early on in our marriage. It was eventually something we had sacrificed to have in order for our children to grow up with a quality instrument. We envisioned it to be something that would set a "tone" or precedent in our home of the importance of music pursuits to our family. Not to mention all the beautiful music we hoped it would eventually bring to our home and family! (Which it did!)

We never imagined that we would adopt a child one day who would benefit immeasurably, even *therapeutically,* from it. Avah not only really enjoyed lying under or beside the grand piano, there were times it was the only thing that would console her distress, such as after a surgery or hospital stay, while weaning off of powerful medications. We wondered if she could somehow feel the vibrations, perhaps through the floor, or in some other sensory way we didn't completely understand... No matter, except that it offered her pleasant, fulfilling distraction from her discomfort.

Then, in 2012, just weeks before her FIRST birthday, she was legally freed and able to be adopted. And so, we became her family forever, and she became Avah Grace.

And there is more.

More Amazing Avah Grace

Our family often made music together, with a variety of instruments, and/or singing. We discovered that with the tune, *Amazing Grace* – she consistently, especially brightened. By her second birthday, she had begun, in her own special way, to *hum* it along with us! She really connected with the music - with us – and *enjoyed* it! This was all very special and important to us, as we collectively felt this enhanced her quality of life… (And ours!)

There wasn't a medical explanation for her obvious *hearing*, or the real social bonds she was forging, or the musical *preferences* she demonstrated. Her delight in the music, an activity that by all understanding, requires brain structures she didn't have – was nothing less than a miracle. Her scans showed her to be left with little more than a brain stem. A "silver lining," as it is called sometimes, as scans show just a hint of upper brain tissue eclipsing the lower/middle part. Without auditory or visual processing centers, or brain structures as you and I have, she wasn't *hearing* or *seeing* the way you and I experience, or even think of these senses. Neither was she cognitively *processing* the way most of us do. And yet – she *did* ALL these things in her own way, or experienced them. At least her own unique version of them. Simply put, Avah continued to amaze us – as much as she continued to baffle her specialists with awe. And she continued to rewrite *the book* on infant brain injury.

In 2016 we celebrated *another* birthday. We sang Amazing Grace WITH her, after seven excited children helped blow out FIVE little candles for a brave little sister-angel they love with all their hearts.

Oh, and that little hymn I first hummed to her (Amazing Grace) – the one she allowed to console her that first time in NICU, the song that enabled, even quickened a deeper connection between her and I – is still her favorite.

So, an astounded, grateful mother again begs the question in her heart, for at least the sixteenth time, who these miracles are really for, and who, after all, is blessing who???

UPDATE 2023

Now, in 2023, our dear sweet Avah, unbelievably, miraculously turned 12 years old!

Of course, everything I explained, described, and divulged in Avah's story above – is now richer, deeper, and just that much more miraculous – to us, and all her continued specialists who, for years now, see her once a year or so (unless otherwise needed). At these routine, annual *get-togethers,* they just smile in awe and admiration of Avah, who literally glows with that plucky kind of courage, and feisty hope that has made all the difference… After all, her unstoppable courage and boundless *hope,* have somehow afforded her a quality of life, despite circumstances that would have otherwise robbed her (and us!) of such a gift.

Purple Crying

In turn, we decided early on to let this experience called *Avah,* draw us into a good fight. One that involves children, and the fastest growing preventable injury of all time. You see, in the beginning, we asked ourselves how we could best help Avah *speak* for herself.

One of the things we felt strongly about early on was being part of an effective movement to advocate and educate on this national problem that was on the rise, and on a fast track to reaching epidemic proportions. We felt that if we could be a part of helping even one child avoid having to endure what Avah did – it was worth it, and that *she* would be all for that, through and through.

And so, we discovered the National Center on Shaken Baby Syndrome, and its Period of Purple Crying program. And then we became avid supporters of it. Eventually, I became a speaker, a co-teacher, and promoter of it at the local, state, and national levels as much as my schedule would allow. Ladies from my church, and other groups, upon our informing and urging on it, and because of their being stirred by Avah and her story – knitted and crocheted literally HUNDREDS of little purple infant hats, which were donated to hospitals all across our region.

The little hats accompanied educational *Purple Crying* material provided by the National Center on Shaken Baby Syndrome that could be given to *ALL* birthing parents, as well as other parents with vulnerable histories, and any other at-risk situations health care or other entities might encounter in our communities. Our entire family felt grateful to be able to promote this material that was hopeful to be *preventive* in nature. Statistics had shown it to help, with much lower incidents of babies returning to hospitals injured when those hospitals' birth-centers embraced the Period of Purple Crying program. We felt so good about this – and knew in our hearts that Avah would be pleased about it, too…

"The Period of PURPLE Crying program is an evidence-based shaken baby syndrome/abusive head trauma (SBS/AHT) prevention program available since 2007. The program has two aims:
1. To support parents and caregivers in their understanding of early increased infant crying
2. To reduce the incidence of SBS/AHT (shaken baby syndrome/abusive head trauma).

The program approaches SBS/AHT and infant abuse prevention by helping parents and caregivers understand the frustrating features of crying in normal, healthy infants that can lead to shaking or abuse. The program provides the opportunity for parents to learn about the crying characteristics from over 50 years of research on normal infant crying conducted by Dr. Ronald G. Barr, and other scientists worldwide." (From the NCSBS Website, link below.)

For more info, to access the training for yourself or someone else, or learn more about getting involved with efforts to reduce this blight upon our nation's children – please see:

https://dontshake.org/purple-crying .

Here is a video that helps explain this horrible thing called Shaken Baby Syndrome. It demonstrates how quickly devastating injuries can happen to children and furthers understanding of the physical dynamics involved with this type of non-accidental trauma – which is a misnomer, as many caregivers do "accidentally" shake a baby. Sometimes at risk, inexperienced, or otherwise vulnerable caregivers are honestly trying to soothe a fussy baby, even being seemingly *affirmed* for their unrealized actions in the early aftermath of injuries with a *"calmer"* baby. In many of these cases, caregivers do not realize how quickly and easily deep brain trauma can occur. Neither do they realize that the "calmness" after abusive shaking is not due to baby soothing but is a *response* to brain injury. *https://bit.ly/3YB0hfF*

The following is an excellent article (which includes the above video).

https://healthresearchfunding.org/shaken-baby-syndrome-statistics/

Disclaimer: Sometimes caregivers get overly anxious or stifled by this alarming information. It's easy to become overwhelmed with an *unnecessary* level of fear to interact with infants even normally. To this, I would like to offer that being a parent or caregiver can certainly be unnerving, even scary – especially for inexperienced parents/caregivers.

However, my advice to you: trust your instincts. Use common sense. Remember, as with anything, practice builds confidence!

Handle <u>with care</u> - but DO HANDLE!

Babies need love, attention, eye contact, caring touch, and consistent, nurturing interaction. These are all *essential* to their well-being and normal development. AND these natural motions assist with *your* attachment to baby as well. This is all part of how your skills with a baby develop, mature, and gain confidence. The point is – caregivers MUST safely touch, hold, rock, cuddle, and snuggle. It is SO IMPORTANT! Just remember:

Be GENTLE. TAKE a BREAK,
NEVER SHAKE!

And, if you think you might know of a worrisome situation where infant abuse could be a risk – please remember AVAH! Remember the information here and DO SOMETHING. Educate yourself on how to help! https://dontshake.org/purple-crying .

Know that many children, including Avah, would have had substantially improved outcomes if help had been sought SOONER. BEFORE an infant is the victim of MULTIPLE injuries, or injuries that worsen due to lack of proper, early treatment for traumatic brain injury.

There are an average of 1300 cases per year in the U.S. of shaken babies – 25% of which result in death, with the rest being left with a range of permanent, mild to devastating disabilities. Just TAKE a BREAK, NEVER SHAKE! And let's *all* help these precious babies everywhere be safer!

~To, for, and on behalf of precious Avah Grace~

~~~~Verily I say unto you, Inasmuch as ye have done it unto one of the least of these my brethren, ye have done it unto me. Matthew 25:40

One more plug, in the spirit of *HOPE*. The kind that makes us *act* in faith, to help realize our goals; please visit the National Center for Shaken Baby Syndrome's site/store – for brochures and other educational materials to help turn the tide of this terrible epidemic…It's also an important, credible, Not-For Profit organization to just outright support with a tax-deductible donation… After all, every injured baby that is *prevented* through these educational efforts - saves countless funds (an immeasurable amount of savings by now, that this organization's valiant efforts have realized for our society).

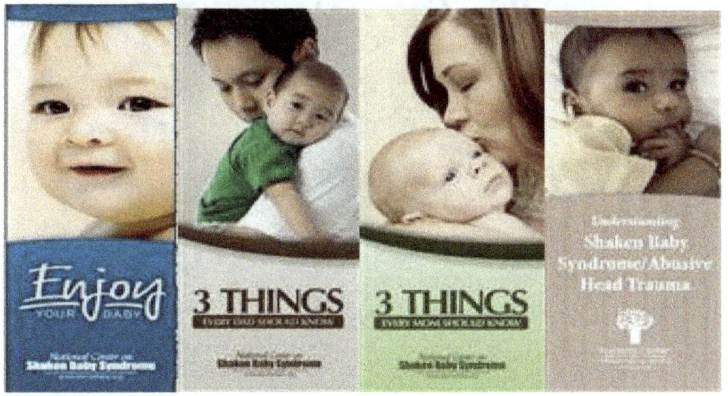

https://bit.ly/3qsiGP8

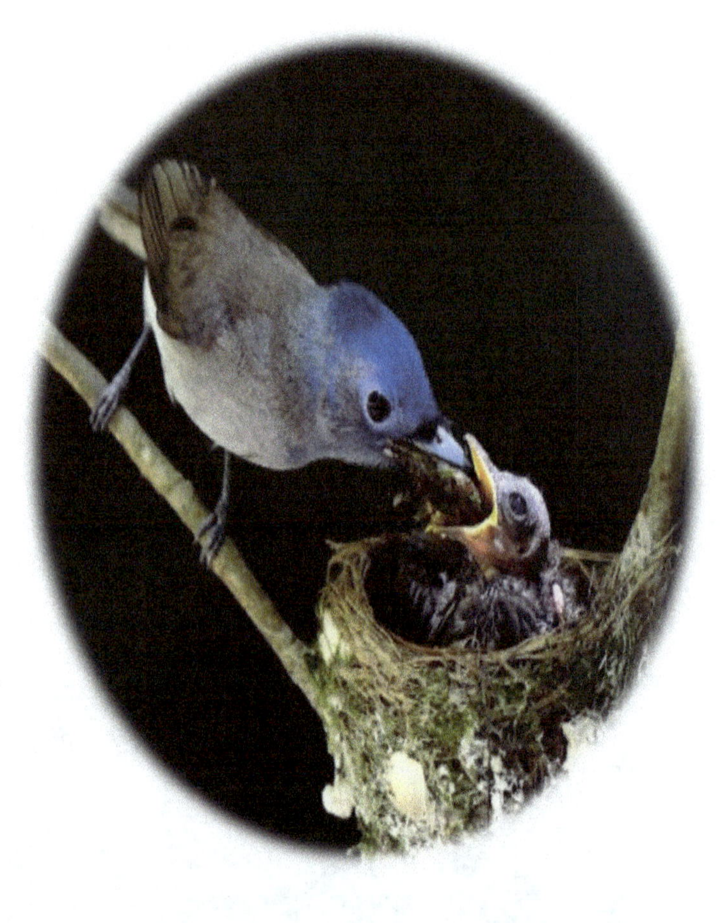

The End

Beauty for Ashes

(A Pebbled Lane Books Mantra)

To appoint unto them
that mourn in Zion, -
To give unto them beauty for ashes,
the oil of joy for mourning,
the garment of praise
for the spirit of heaviness;
that they might be called
trees of righteousness,
the planting of the Lord,
that he might be glorified.

Isaiah 61:3 (KJV)

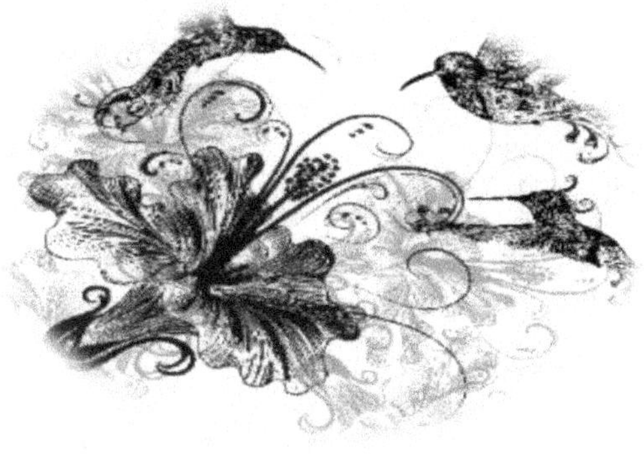

About the Author
Connie Kerbs

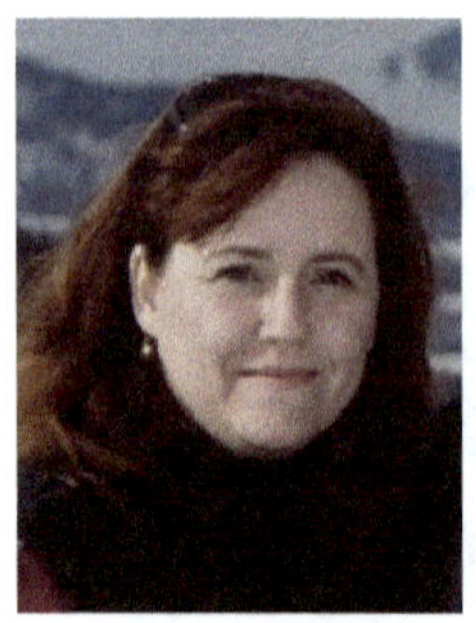

Connie, nudged to write by her inner muse since early childhood, is thrilled to see her life-long dream of authoring come to fruition. Her stories and poems have been published in several books and magazines. Her Pebbled Lane Books series, (FINE Reads Press), offers a variety of thematic series and titles that contribute inspiration and entertainment to the contemporary literary landscape.

She lives with her high-school sweetheart husband of 35 years in their cozy house in the woodsy mountains of the Inland Northwest where they enjoy their dogs, cats, a dozen backyard chickens - and the several still home of their unique family (in size, composition, and volume).

Being blessed with three biological children in the middle of a 30-year run as specialized foster/adopt parents which led to several "miracle," adoptions, Mrs. Kerbs says has, "honed and humbled us all as it has bathed us in bliss."

When not writing or mothering her unique family she is likely nature-fixing or collecting eggs. To find more on author, Connie Kerbs, and her growing body of work, please visit: **www.ConnieKerbs.com**

About Pebbled Lane Books

"Every journey of a thousand miles begins with one small step..."

The narratives and verse selected for the Pebbled Lane

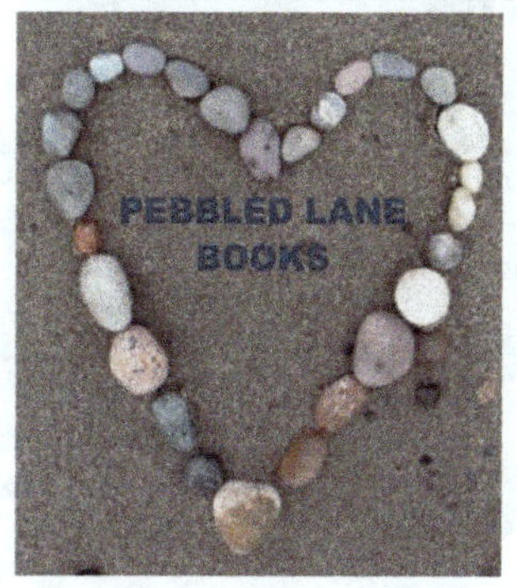

Books Series are like the pocket full of pebbles we've each curiously eyed and randomly plucked from a path or a beach littered with them.

They are intriguing little stones, each with their own unique characteristics and complex, even mysterious backstory. Pebble lovers everywhere will appreciate the variety, the "stuff of life," that Pebbled Lane Books are made of.

The imprint complements the mission of its publisher, F.I.N.E. Reads Press, offering engaging, thematic works that are as encouraging and uplifting as they are entertaining. The collection offers a variety of hearty reading experiences, which are all part of an exciting, enduring, and enlightening body of work. For more, please visit:
www.PebbledLaneBooks.com

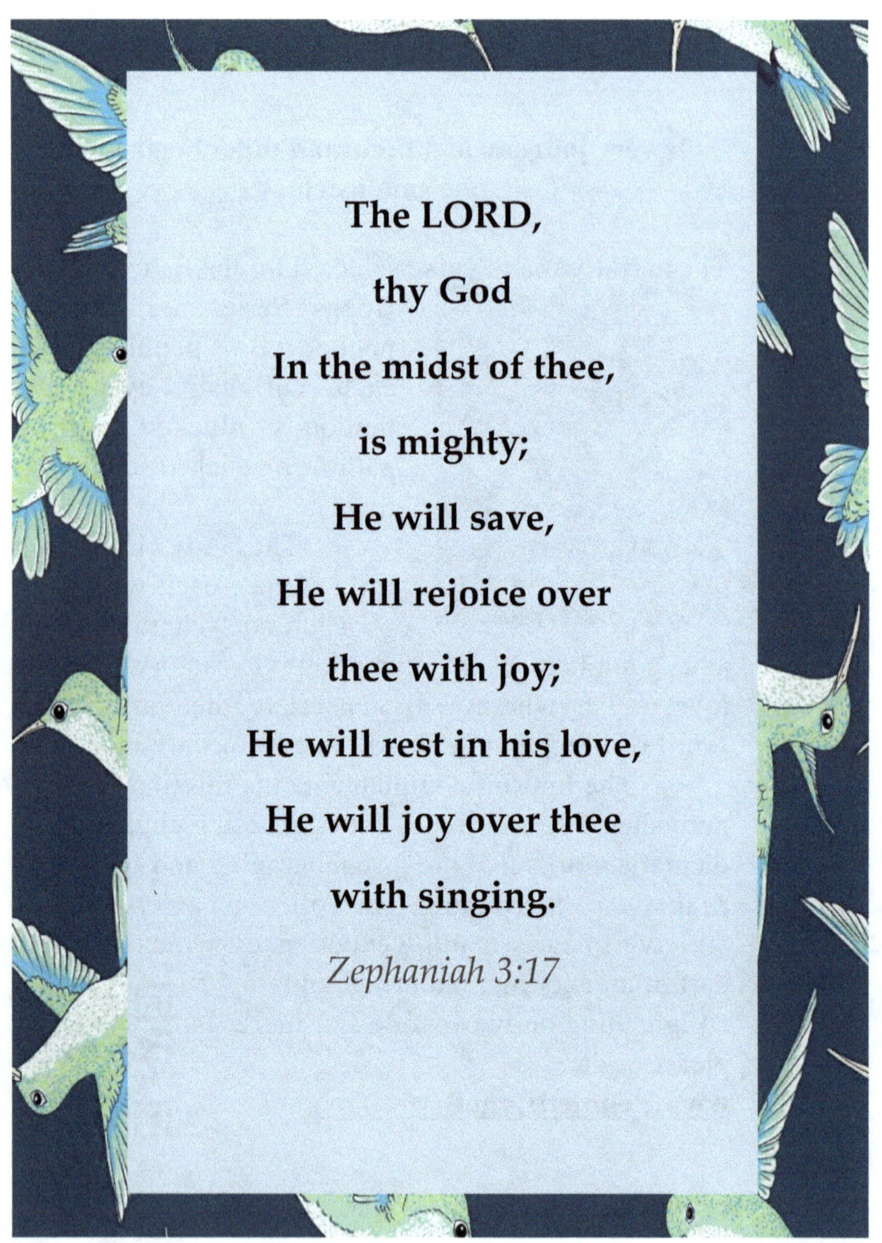

The LORD,

thy God

In the midst of thee,

is mighty;

He will save,

He will rejoice over

thee with joy;

He will rest in his love,

He will joy over thee

with singing.

Zephaniah 3:17

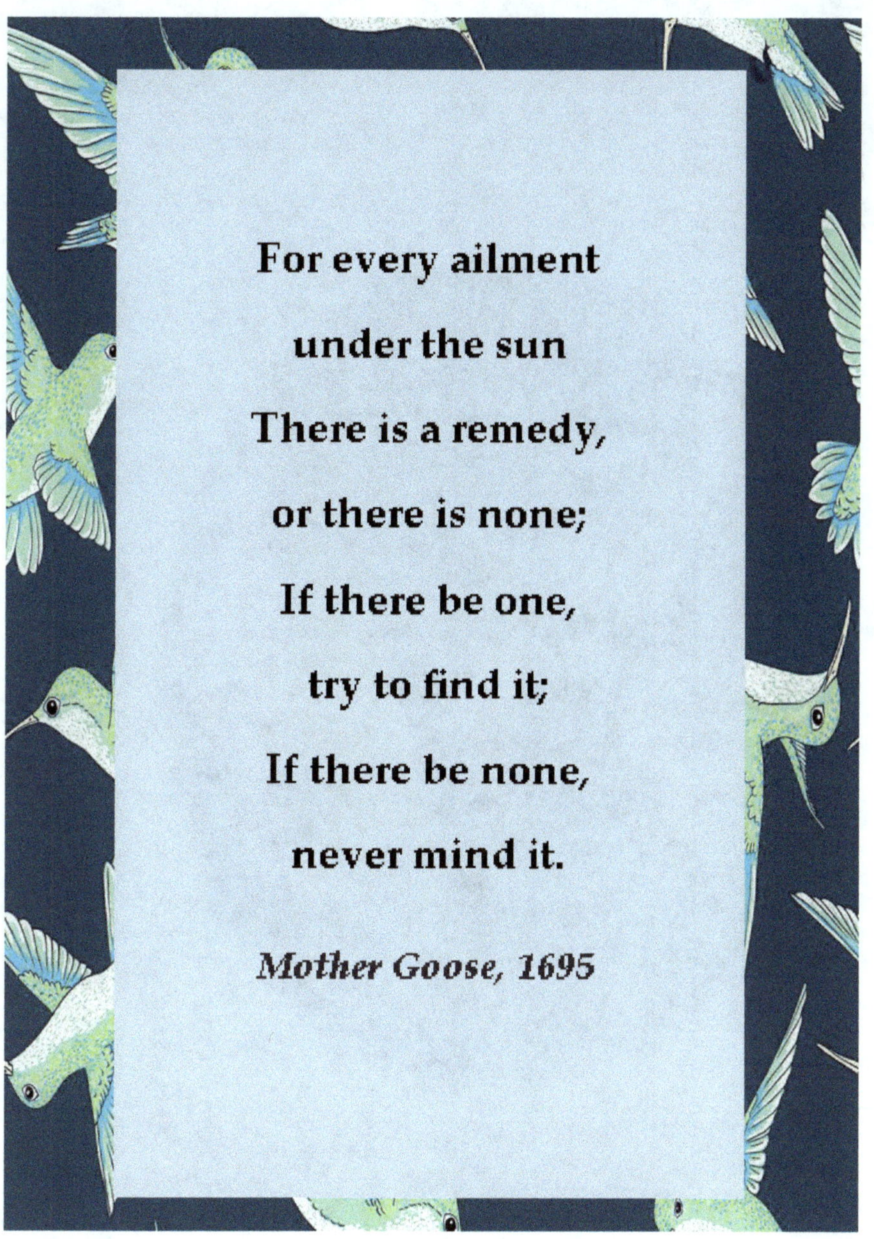
For every ailment
under the sun
There is a remedy,
or there is none;
If there be one,
try to find it;
If there be none,
never mind it.
Mother Goose, 1695

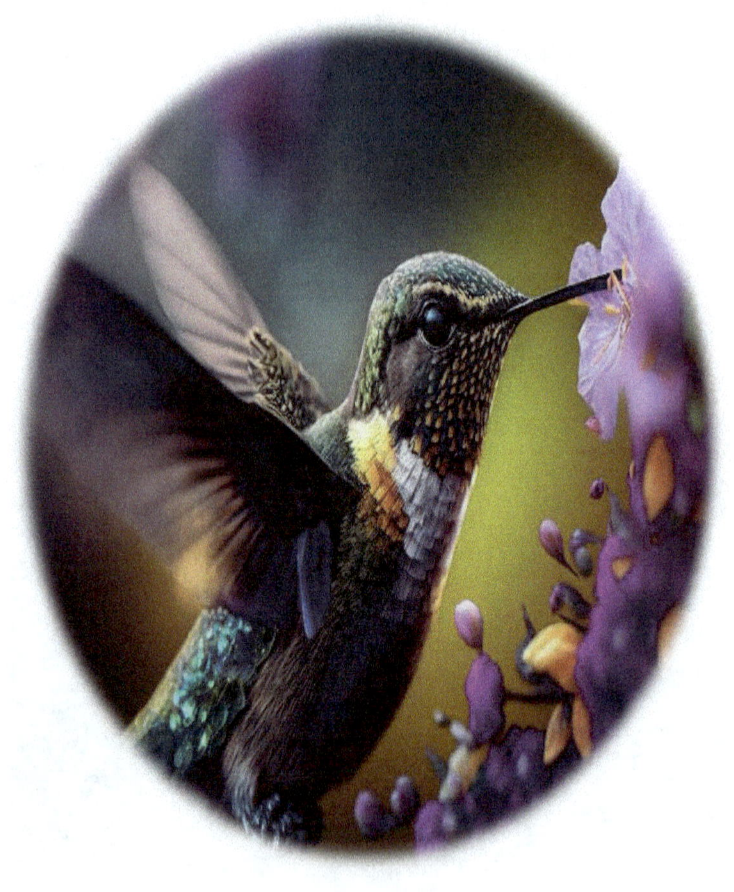

Pebbled Lane Books
by
Connie Kerbs

Book 1 of
Vera's Verses:
Whatsoever Things

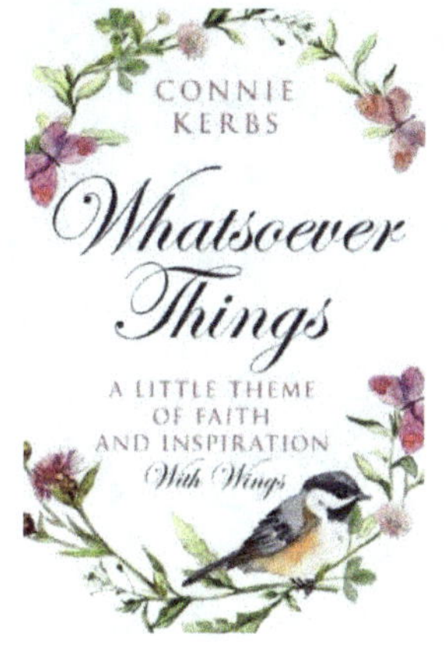

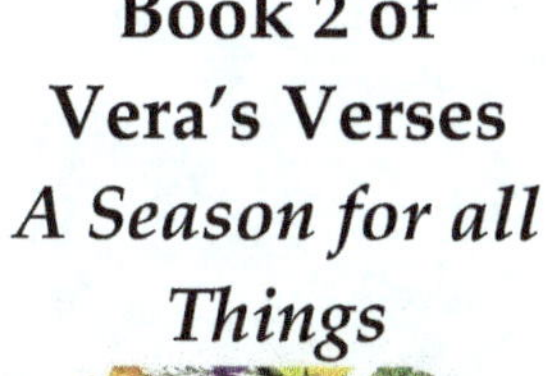

Book 2 of
Vera's Verses
A Season for all
Things

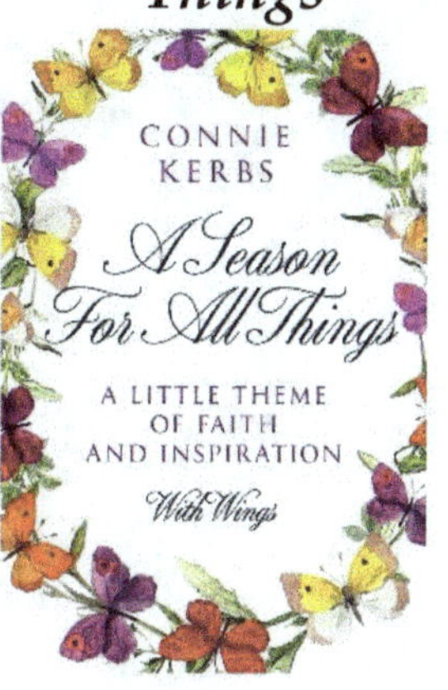

www.pebbledlanebooks.com

www.conniekerbs.com

amzn.to/3YqdqH1

www.ingramcontent.com/pod-product-compliance
Lightning Source LLC
LaVergne TN
LVHW050534100826
845148LV00002B/550

* 9 7 8 1 7 3 6 7 4 1 9 4 8 *